# JOSEPH BENNETT
# OF EVANS

Also by Kevin H. Siepel:

Rebel: The Life and Times of
John Singleton Mosby

*Courtesy David Ritchie Carr*

Joseph Bennett

# JOSEPH BENNETT OF EVANS

## AND THE

# GROWING OF NEW YORK'S NIAGARA FRONTIER

## KEVIN H. SIEPEL

**Spruce Tree Press**

Angola, New York

# Joseph Bennett of Evans
## and the Growing of New York's Niagara Frontier

by Kevin H. Siepel

Published by:
**Spruce Tree Press**
PO Box 21
Angola, NY 14006

website:   http://www.sprucetreepress.com
e-mail:    sales@sprucetreepress.com

Published 2006

ISBN-13   978-0-9786466-1-5 (paperback)
ISBN-10   0-9786466-1-4 (paperback)

Library of Congress Control Number:  2006905847

### Publisher's Cataloging-in-Publication

Siepel, Kevin H.
   Joseph Bennett of Evans and the growing of New York's
Niagara Frontier / Kevin H. Siepel.
   p. cm.
   Includes bibliographical references and index.
   ISBN 0-9786466-1-4

   1. Bennett, Joseph, 1803-1899.  2. Evans (N.Y. :
Town)--Social life and customs.  3. Evans (N.Y. : Town)
--History--19th century.  4. Niagara Frontier (N.Y.)--
Social life and customs.  5. Niagara Frontier (N.Y.)--
History--19th century.  6. New York (State)--History,
Local.   I. Title.

   F123.S54 2006            974.7'9603'092
                            QBI06-600264

Cover design by Karen Ross, www.KarenRoss.com
Cover photos courtesy of Battle of Plattsburgh Association, Town of Evans Historical Society, and Chittenango Landing Canal Boat Museum

This book is printed on acid-free paper.

To young people.

That they might understand
that others
have been here before them

*After leaving Cold Springs and arriving at the top of the hill, I had a full view of Buffalo and Lake Erie . . . I just thought I never saw anything so beautiful. The village nestling at the foot of Main and two or three parallel streets. The broad and beautiful lake, a topsail schooner sailing up the bay. Weather fine, everything seemed combined to make it enchanting to me.*

Joseph Bennett on his first sight of Buffalo, June 1820, age 16

# CONTENTS

Photographs follow pages 82, 140, and 180

# PREFACE

New York state's Niagara Frontier has produced its share of people worth writing about. The list is long, ranging from scientists to senators, from actors and actresses to athletes and artists, from journalists to inventors, and from soldiers to business leaders, jurists, and clergy. To begin to make such a list would be to court disaster, since surely some worthy would be left out.

The list of those from Erie County's Town of Evans who merit attention—whether for internationally, nationally, or locally significant accomplishments—is more manageable. There was Willis Carrier, for example, the inventor of the air conditioner; there was Pius Schwert, civic leader, major league ballplayer, and congressman; there was Hiram Backus, a colorful character and consummate showman. There have been others.

But off in the background there has always been Joseph Bennett, a man responsible for no recognized inventions, who played no role on the national stage, and who does not appear to have had a high-octane personality. Bennett was an ordinary man who wore many hats. He was a farmer, construction contractor, businessman, public servant, and a religious and family man who—despite his ordinariness—was not unknown in western New York state.

Bennett's life, launched in August 1803, would stretch from Lewis and Clark's exploration of the west to the Wright Brothers' experiments with flying machines, from the War of 1812 to the war against Spain, from the presidency of Jefferson to that of McKinley, from America as wilderness to America as budding world power.

Young Joseph found himself within earshot of the 1814 naval engagement between American and British forces on Lake Champlain. He arrived in the village of

Buffalo less than a decade after its burning by the British. As a young man he participated in the building of the Erie Canal and the Pennsylvania canal system. He was in Buffalo when Lincoln passed through en route to his destiny in Washington. He served as assemblyman in Albany, and was a frequently reelected town supervisor. He was active all his life in church affairs. Bennett headed up the mid-nineteenth century equivalent of Erie County Social Services, and served as chairman of the Erie County Board of Supervisors, roughly equivalent to the County Executive of today. On his property he founded a business that gave people great pleasure, that provided financial security for himself and his descendants, and that outlived him by many years.

With all this it remains difficult to "see" Joseph Bennett. We have few pictures of him and few independent sources that mention him. Because such outside sources on Joseph Bennett are scarce, his life is not amenable to traditional biography, and this book should not be viewed as such. We have little evidence of how Bennett was seen by his contemporaries, even by his own family.

But the evidence we do have is valuable and illuminating, for Bennett did something that many of his better-known contemporaries did not do: he left behind a journal, a window on his world, a window from which we can view, through his eyes, nearly all of the nineteenth century.

The story that follows is in fact a story, not an annotation of Bennett's jottings. It is the story of the development of western New York and early America as seen through the prism of Bennett's experience. It is not a bare timeline of Joseph Bennett's days, but rather a tale of how Bennett's days fit into the tide of life around him in his town, county, region, state, and nation. It is, principally, the story of how this man participated in the growing of America, and, in particular, the growing of New York state's Niagara Frontier.

To paraphrase Bennett family descendant Joseph C. Anderson II, who has carried out considerable genealogical research on the Bennett family: at one level Bennett has presented us with a personal account of nine decades of one man's life; at a deeper level he has chronicled the evolution of a small town in rural America from its beginnings in log huts to today's vacation homes; and at the deepest level he has left us a series of invaluable snapshots of the history and development of our nation.

I hope my distillation of these days long past encourages awareness that we today are caretakers rather than owners of our community, our world, and our times. Others created, built, and enjoyed before us, and still others will labor and bask in the summer suns of tomorrow.

May these future generations remember us, just as we pause to consider this generation long departed.

Kevin H. Siepel
Angola-on-the-Lake, New York

# 1

# GETTING TO THE WEST

It had been a long and circuitous journey for the young Vermonter, for his parents Samuel and Sally, and for his seven younger siblings, and the future was anything but clear. On this summer's day in the village of Buffalo in 1820 he could not have known that the wild land on the edge of this great water that so impressed him would be his home for the remainder of a long and fruitful life.

Chelsea, in the interior of Vermont, had been the birthplace of Joseph Bennett nearly 17 years previous. On August 8, 1803, he was born the eldest of what would eventually be a family of 10 children. His father was of the "sturdy Green Mountain race," and his mother of "Puritan stock." Both Sally and Samuel were born during the War for Independence. Samuel, who seemed capable of learning any trade, is first encountered, in Vermont, working as a bookbinder. "My father," recalled Bennett, "was a man of small means, but was strictly honest and of unqualified integrity."

"My mother," he continued, "was an active, energetic Christian, faithful and lovely, and untiring in her devotion to her family."

As a very young child, Joseph was frail. Methods of strengthening children then differed greatly from today. "I well remember," said Bennett, my father taking me, every other morning, out of bed just after daylight, carrying to a cold stream, just under the foot of the Green Mountain, and wading to a sufficient depth, then dipping me. How I did cling to my father and beg not to be put in the water, but after being wrapped in a woolen blanket I felt splendidly.

This dipping treatment, he recalled, continued for three weeks.

A religious man all his life, Joseph began his religious formation in the Presbyterian Church. "I remember," he wrote,

going [at the age of four, in about 1807] with my parents on a very cold day, sat in pews like pens, half the congregation with back to the Minister. Every family carried a foot stove or we should all have perished, it being excessively cold, and the Minister read his sermon *about two hours long* and no warmth in it, *so they said.* Never any fire in the Meeting House. I don't know but it would, at that time been considered an unpardonable sin to establish one.

He attended classes in an old schoolhouse with a large fireplace at each end, with "fires large enough to roast an ox." Frequently as many as 70 scholars filled the room, with two teachers. "Each family sent a large lunch for their own children," he wrote, "of good wholesome Yankee food, Indian bread, ham, dried beef, sausage, and nutcakes."

In March 1810, Samuel Bennett sold his property in Vermont and moved his pregnant wife and three children (Joseph, Rhoda, and Alonzo)[1] across the Green Mountains and Lake Champlain to the Town of Jay, in Essex County, New York. The crossing of the mountains was made difficult enough by wet snow and cold, but at the edge of the 125-mile-long lake that separates Vermont from New York, where a lengthy crossing had to be

---

[1] Rhoda had been born in 1805 or 1806, and Alonzo in 1807.

made, conditions were more serious. "As we came down the mountain," wrote Joseph,

> . . . it was very warm and found the water over the ice on the lake from two to five inches deep . . . The inhabitants said there was no danger, that the ice was very thick. We had either to cross the lake or stay there a long time. While my father was in a quandary, a man came along with a team and said he should go. My father said he would follow and did so. My mother was terribly afraid. We went over all safe, landed at Peru, I think four or five miles above [i.e., south of] Plattsburgh and from Peru to Jay, . . . some 14 miles in a southerly direction.

Joseph's father, who seems to have had ready cash from the sale of his Vermont property, purchased land on the rushing Ausable River and commenced setting up a water-powered factory for carding wool and making clothing. It would be the first in this part of the country. Wool from sheared sheep would be thoroughly cleaned by the owner, oiled and greased with lard, butter, or some other soft grease, then tied up in blankets or sheets to be brought to the carding works for machine-combing into rolls. The content of these rolls would then be spun into yarn, later to be woven into cloth. In those days, noted Joseph, a woman was paid 75 cents a week for spinning.

Samuel Bennett began setting up his carding and clothier works in the spring of 1811. The building must have been there already, for by summertime the business was in full operation. In November, however, he suffered a calamity, one from which he never seemed to recover: in that month his new plant burned to the ground. And, as if that were not enough, Providence saw fit to frown on him even more sternly: a few days after the fire, the family's new home—under construction at the time—was leveled by a tornado.

"My father now was utterly discouraged," recalled Joseph, at the time eight years old. "Was left very poor with a family of wife and five small children [Joseph, Rhoda, Alonzo, Sarah, and Samuel]."[2]  Samuel began immediately to build another house, but his livelihood had been destroyed, and his spirit doubtless battered. To make matters worse, the land was about to be invaded by a foreign army: Essex County was on the verge of becoming the eastern wing of the arena where the nation would fight its second war against Britain.

Like many fathers before and since, Samuel Bennett did everything he could to keep his family going through bad times, made worse now by the fledgling United States government's shocking declaration of war (in June 1812) against the greatest power of Europe. The winter of 1813-14 found Samuel in the U.S. military camps around Plattsburgh, a huckster. Ten-year-old Joseph was at his side. "During that time," wrote Joseph,

> I learned to drum, taught by the army drummers. During the summer I was at home in Jay, a part of the time I was drummer at a recruiting station in the village . . . The constant talk was *War, War.* The two navies on Lake Champlain were arming and preparing, with great perseverance and energy, for the coming encounter.

As 1814 progressed, he said, "the inhabitants in that region were under excitement and fear of the Indians. The British army was hovering over our northern frontier with their Indian allies, and threats were made that they would be let loose upon the unoffending inhabitants."

In Canada, Lieutenant General Sir George Prevost, son of a Swiss mercenary who had helped control Georgia for England during the war for American independence, was preparing, with a new infusion of troops from Britain—hardened veterans, fresh from victory over the French—to put an end to this bothersome conflict. He would mount a strong overland attack, supported by a

---

[2] Sarah was born in 1810, probably in Jay, and Samuel in 1811, in Jay.

fleet on Lake Champlain. Following this action—whose issue was not the least bit in doubt—the ships of this fleet would carry the invaders south to winter at the head of the lake, from which point they would then move against New York, Baltimore, and Washington.[3]

U.S. Major General George Izard, well aware of the coming invasion from the north, was preparing his 6,000 poorly equipped men—largely raw recruits—at Plattsburgh for the expected assault: training, digging in, positioning arms, men, and supplies as rapidly as possible. Believing his troops incapable of withstanding the invasion expected via the Richelieu River, Lake Champlain, and Plattsburgh, he enlisted the assistance of 30-year-old Navy Lieutenant Thomas Macdonough, Master Commandant on Lake Champlain. Naval support on the army's right flank, it was thought, would be of key importance in blocking the invasion.

In August, with the War Department in Washington now deceived by disinformation from Canada that the main invasion would be not via Lake Champlain, but via Niagara, Izard was ordered to take 4,500 troops to meet the perceived threat on the western frontier, an order he obeyed with great misgiving. The defense of Lake Champlain and the water route to the Middle States would be left to newly minted Brigadier General Alexander Macomb, who was left with 1,500 ragtag troops augmented by 700 militia. Many of Macomb's men were invalids who could fight only from static positions.

Once past Macomb's patched-together force and Macdonough's ships, no regular army formation that might oppose Prevost would be found from Plattsburgh to Baltimore.

On September 1, following the departure of Izard's forces, the vanguard of 15,000 seasoned British regulars appeared at Rouses Point at the northern end of the

---

[3] Battle details taken largely from David Fitz-Enz, "September 11 1814," *Military Illustrated*, September 2002, no. 172: 24-31.

lake, and by September 6 the land battle was being gradually joined.

As the two sides maneuvered for advantage along Plattsburgh's Saranac River, the British fleet, unready to fight and strapped for trained men, remained at Rouses Point drilling gun crews and rushing to complete on-board construction. By September 11, however, the Royal Navy had appeared off Plattsburgh to engage Macdonough's ships, which were anchored in line, waiting.

Macdonough, a veteran of action against the North African pirates, had been feverishly readying—even building—ships on Lake Champlain. (The brig *Eagle* was built in 19 days.) But since, like the British, he did not have enough trained men to crew them, he had commandeered several hundred of Macomb's already weakened force to do so. All feared that the lack of specialized skills among the landsmen would make for a poor naval effort. The likelihood of a poor effort on land was taken for granted. Plattsburgh promised to be a mere bump in the road for the British on their way to Baltimore and Washington.

"About the first of September," wrote Joseph,

> all able-bodied men, in that region, that were able to bear arms were called to Plattsburgh to strengthen our forces . . . On the 11th inst., the decisive battle was fought . . . The land forces fought at Plattsburgh, the Navy on Lake Champlain, both in sight of each other . . . What a day it was to the helpless women, children, and old men in the little villages and region round about. The booming of cannon distinctly heard nearly twenty miles away.

Due not only to Macdonough's superior tactics, but also to a series of small disasters that befell the British fleet—a single cannon shot that killed its commanding officer, for example, a wind that drove the fleet directly into the muzzles of American cannon, a ship run aground—the British warships one after another struck their colors. With the battle on the water lost, Prevost would be able to transport his army no further, and despite a still tenable land position, he ordered his forces back to Canada.[4]

Eleven-year-old Joseph and his family and townspeople did not know what was happening. They had barricaded themselves in a large timber blockhouse in the village, and "under the command of an old Revolutionary soldier," garrisoned it with women and old men, all armed "with every kind of weapon," ready to die "by Indian massacre." But, remembered Joseph, "as excitement was at its highest pitch, a horseman came at full speed, swinging his hat shouting, '*The victory is ours, the victory is ours, the enemy fleeing, British fleet destroyed*'."

♧

Whether related to this close brush with war or simply in response to a promising opportunity, Samuel Bennett sold what was left of his property later that month and moved his family back to Vermont, this time to Vergennes, and this time via sloop and bateau instead of by perilous ice crossing. He would be taking over the management of a large distillery.

The Treaty of Ghent, ending the war with Britain, was signed two months later, on Christmas Eve 1814. The news of the signing did not arrive in time to prevent the slaughter, mostly of British troops, at New Orleans. "A telegraph," wrote Joseph, "would have saved all that bloodshed."

Following a brief move to yet another Vermont town, Samuel collected his family once again and headed now to the far west—Union Springs, New York, on the shores of Cayuga Lake.[5] It was June 1816, "the year without a summer," so cold was it throughout North America (due

---

[4] A subsequent naval court of inquiry found Prevost to blame for the loss of this battle. He requested a court martial to vindicate himself, but died before the court martial could be convened.
[5] The presence of Sally Bennett's brother Jonathan in Union Springs may have explained this choice.

to lingering atmospheric ash from a volcanic eruption the previous year in modern-day Indonesia). Joseph's father established himself again in the distillery business. "At that time," recalled Joseph, eventually a temperance booster himself, "the business was laudable and honorable. All classes of people used alcohol as a beverage."

Joseph, now nearly 13, got a job clerking for Samuel Williams & Co., owners of general stores around Cayuga Lake. From these three Quaker brothers he received no salary, but his board and a clothing allowance only. He was delighted with his situation, where he was given the chance to exercise his growing sense of responsibility. One of the absolutely happiest aspects of the job for him was the chance to acquire and develop a skill that he would cherish into old age—driving a boat under sail. On the shores of this 40-mile long lake just west of today's Syracuse, the company had three stores—one on the eastern shore at Union Springs, one on the lake's western shore, and one at its head in the south. Roads being extremely primitive in 1816, and canals and railroads existing only on paper, the stores were supplied by boat.

"Our company," explained Joseph, "owned one schooner of 60 tons, one of 30 tons, 2 or 3 river boats that were manned with 7 men each, one sloop of 10 tons, and two sail boats." The schooners were used to carry "land plaster" (i.e., finely ground gypsum, used chiefly as fertilizer) from quarries near Union Springs to the store at the head of the lake, then to return north laden with lumber. Taking advantage of the network of navigable streams such as the Seneca River and Wood Creek, the three shallow-draft boats traveled northeast into Oneida Lake, and as far east as Albany and back. The sailboats were, like gnats, in constant motion across the lake surface, hauling goods to the stores as needed, and taking passengers on weekend pleasure excursions.

"It was soon discovered," wrote Joseph, "that I had a special taste, and talent, for sailing and navigation. When I was only 16 years old, was called the best sailor in the crowd, although my bosses were from Rhode Island, and two of them were good sailors."

By this time, three more children had been added to the Bennett household—Thomas, Laban, and Lucina.[6] "All healthy and smart," remarked the eldest of the eight. Joseph gave his parents some relief by not living at home, but with his employers.

"My head quarters," he wrote, "was in the store at Union Springs but am often sent to the store across the lake in Seneca City, frequently to take charge of the store for weeks, and then perhaps sent with goods in a boat to the other stores." With the joy of a carefree 16-year-old, this kind of business was "just glorious" to him.

Another activity that he appears to have considered "glorious" was ice-skating. "The ice during the winter season on Cayuga Lake," he said, "is generally very enjoyable for skating and ice-boating. Frequently one hundred or more can be seen on skates in an evening."

"Very seldom," he hastened to add, "any one drowned."

Attracted throughout his life to adventures on winter ice, he took chances.

One day in December 1818, Dr. Satterlee and myself being anxious to cross the lake. The lake from each shore being strong enough to bear for a mile or more, then a streak of water in the middle. We took a light skiff, pushed it before us until it broke in and passed over the water and onto the ice, the other side. That night was a very severe cold night. The next morning we put on skates and crossed the lake home to the east side. In crossing we kept about two rods apart

---

[6] Thomas was born in August 1814 in Jay, the month before the battle on Lake Champlain; Laban in 1816 or 1817 in Union Springs; and Lucina about 1818, also in Union Springs. Two more children would be born to the Bennetts within the next five years: Valentine in the Town of Evans in March 1821 and Caroline, also in Evans, May 1823. Sally Bennett was about 44 when Caroline was born.

side and side, the ice bent so much we dare not get nearer.

"It was an awfully *foolhardy, reckless act*," he concluded, "only a wonder we were not lost."

Thin ice was not the only danger he faced. Powder kegs were a fact of life in 1819, their contents used for blasting as well as for weapons. The Williams brothers sold black powder in their store, which provided Joseph with another opportunity to shorten his life. "One evening while in the store," he wrote,

> I took a candle, went into the loft after some article kept there. A keg of powder, or a keg half full of powder, stood up there with the head out, *open*. In passing around, the candle accidentally fell out of the candlestick into the powder. "*Thoughts run rappidly* [sic] *in emergency*." I snatched the candle out instantly from the powder still burning, in half a second after the candle was out of the keg, snap, snap, went the powder in the wick of the candle. Wasn't that an escape. I think I was light complexion about that time.

The year 1819 brought bad times—the first major financial "panic" in the United States. By the spring of 1820, Joseph's father had had enough and once again packed up the family to head west, this time to Niagara County, New York. He intended to remain there only a few months before moving on, probably to the Western Reserve, in northeast Ohio. Samuel did not take his eldest son, who was still needed by the Williams brothers, with him. The Williams brothers would not, however, need him for long, because they were soon put out of business by the national financial crisis. Joseph said goodbye to his employers in June and followed his family's path, spending a night and nearly two days on the bruising stage westward to Buffalo. (He notes in passing the presence of young Buffalo congressman Albert H. Tracy as a fellow passenger.)

# Getting to the West

"I found my father, mother and family all right," he recalled, "eight miles out from Buffalo on the Williamsville Road in the Town of Amherst."

Joseph acclimated himself quickly to his life's new rhythm and to his neighbors. He was impressed by the Germans he met everywhere—"a jolly lot of people they are"—and he mixed easily with the younger among them, ready for any adventure. A few days after his arrival, with little else to do, he accepted an invitation from a half-dozen young Germans to head to Buffalo with them (in horse-drawn wagons) to attend a trial that promised to be a sensation—a Methodist minister from Lancaster on trial for "a very immoral crime." The trip would prove to be more memorable than the trial. "Soon after leaving home," he recounted,

> the Dutch inaugurated a race, with whipping, laughing and shouting. The race was exciting, *roads rough and stumpy*. About five miles out of Buffalo, we overtook another Dutchman with a yoke of oxen and waggon, without a box, he sitting upon the hind axeltree [sic]. The spirit entered into him, determined not to leave the track, or be passed, commenced whipping and yelling like the others. The oxen became frightened and run as oxen can run, with a vengeance, and fairly outstripped the horses. Soon run foul a stump, tore the waggon apart, left the hind wheels and the man at the stump, the man bleeding but not killed. Oxen brought up at Cold Springs. There the race ended.

Following their day in Buffalo, as he wrote, the young men "returned home . . . in better order than [they] came." (The minister was found guilty and sentenced to 12 years in prison.)

About July 1, Bennett determined that he had to see western New York's most famous attraction, so he rode a horse from Williamsville to Niagara Falls. "There was no way," he explained, "to get down below the falls, only by a frail, rickety, cheap stairway, that appeared very much unsafe. I however ventured down and back. Did not see a single person there, except a few that lived there, went back home at night."

Accustomed from his years of working with the Williams brothers to being busy, the nearly 17-year-old boy was unhappy with nothing useful to do. He hoped that "some time the wheel would turn" and bring him up.

An opportunity for haying presented itself. "Had never worked an hour in the hayfield in my life, but would try," he said. He worked for a Mr. Hersee, "a well-to-do Dutchman," and had his eyes opened to another side of his new neighbors' culture. Mr. Hersee's wife, he noted, was "rather a sad appearing woman, not very strong, with no help in the house."

> She would get breakfast for five men, after breakfast would come into the hayfield and work until 11 o'clock. Get dinner for the men. After dinner, while the men lay around and smoke, for one hour, she was washing dishes and clearing up, in time to go out again with the men. That seemed to be the Dutch custom. *Abominable.*

When not working, Joseph fell into new pastimes. "I am not blessed with much of a hunting or gunning spirit," he said.

> But during the months of July and August and September, the whole country litterally [sic] swarmed with black squirrels. I saw lots of them in the village of Buffalo, upon dwelling houses and other buildings, almost everyone shooting squirrels. I entered into the spirit also.

Samuel Bennett had by this time taken to farming on shares. His agricultural arena was the Slossen farm, two miles from Williamsville on the main road to Buffalo. Joseph helped his father, but Samuel was not cut out for farming, and the urge to move was again strong on him. By November, he had determined that the time had come to move his family to the Western Reserve.

# Getting to the West

The routine was by now familiar: they loaded the family wagon with all the possessions they had room for, then hitched up "an excellent team of horses" and headed west to Buffalo and out the Lake Erie shoreline for the long trip to Ohio. Sally Bennett was five months pregnant with her ninth child, Valentine.

It was an unusual day for November, remembered Joseph, weather "warm, cloudy, and sultry." By late morning, Buffalo was behind them, and they moved out onto the beach, where, despite the difficulty of driving a heavy wagon over rocks and through sand and shallow water, traveling was far easier than on the lake shore "road." But the journey was arduous in the extreme. The party "traveled up the shore in deep dry sand," reported Joseph, "every man, woman, and child on foot. We tugged through streams, over rocks and boulders all day." He continued:

> Log house taverns every two miles and sometimes oftener, had to leave the beach to get to them. Generally we leave the waggons on the beach and take the teams up to feed.

> Towards night the horses were getting very tired, so concluded to stop at the next hotel. Soon came in sight of a house supposing it to be a tavern, came to it, and found an empty house, evidently had been occupied and used as a log house tavern.

> Our horses were *tired*, we were all *tired*, not knowing how far to the next place, concluded to stop and occupy for the night, which we did. Selected our own rooms and fared sumptuously.

> That night, about midnight, a terrible gale suddenly burst upon us such as I never experienced before. The spray from the lake wet the house like a hard beating rain. It turned very cold before morning, and the house covered with ice, also trees, bushes, land, everything. The gale continued through the next day, and the cold increased. We found plenty of wood and kept warm.

# Joseph Bennett

The next night, the wind began to lull, but very cold. Were now thinking of making a move onward, as our Commissary department needed attention.

While getting ready for a start, Mr. Aaron Salisbury came to the house, and gave us our reckoning. We found we were on the Holland Purchase, State of N.Y., County of Niagara, Town of Eden, 20 miles from Buffalo, at the mouth of the two Sister Creeks, on the shore of Lake Erie.

In modern terms, the family had finished their day's journey in the Town of Evans, Erie County, neither jurisdiction having been erected yet. They found themselves on the windswept beach of a roaring Lake Erie, watching waves rush far up the wet sand to the windrow of ice-encased driftwood that marked high water from the recent storm. They were near the mouth of Little Sister Creek (in those days just yards from the mouth of Big Sister Creek), west of present-day Wendt Beach.

They would soon be convinced to end their journey here.

# 2

# *THE NIAGARA FRONTIER*

Only two generations prior to the Bennetts' arrival in western New York state the area was an unrelieved wilderness, unsurveyed, occupied by native peoples of shifting loyalties and unpredictable passions, the land contested and fought over by Europe's two dominant powers. These lands were then, tenuously, part of New France, with the mouth of the Niagara River of the utmost strategic importance to the French, who could prevent British entry into the whole of the upper Great Lakes by controlling traffic through this strait. To achieve this control, the French in 1726 had constructed a stone fort at the mouth of the Niagara (today's French Castle at Fort Niagara), and in the mid-1750s, as England's menace grew, put enormous effort into enlarging the installation and improving its defenses. In 1759, however, the British succeeded in taking the fort, and from there proceeded to add not only the region surrounding the upper Great Lakes, but more than half of North America, including all of Canada, to their considerable colonial holdings.

Fort Niagara remained in British hands even after the colonies' successful war for independence from Britain, not being ceded to the fledgling United States until 1796 (by Jay's Treaty).

Sixteen years following this treaty, with a U.S. administration that seriously intended to annex Canada, with national feelings still raw on both sides, and with tensions especially high between the U.S. and Royal Navies, Britain and its former colonies again clashed in the war whose reverberations had been felt so strongly by the Bennetts near Plattsburgh. While young Joseph was drumming in the Lake Champlain camps, Fort Niagara was retaken by British forces, and in the dead of winter, December 1813 (in retaliation for American outrages in Canada), the rude village of Buffalo was put to the torch by British troops. It was but six years prior to the Bennetts' arrival that the British had been driven back, by force of arms and subsequent treaty, across the Niagara into Canada, yet Buffalo, when the Bennetts arrived, had already been rebuilt, and was well on the path to gentility.

The first known inhabitants of these lands bordering Lake Erie had been the Neuter (or Kahquah) and Erie tribes, gradually to be supplanted by the Seneca—the westernmost tribe of the Haudenosaunee, or Iroquois, Confederacy, known as the Keepers of the Western Door. In the mid-eighteenth-century contest for supremacy in North America between the great powers of Europe, the Seneca, who by now had displaced the former tribes along Lake Erie's eastern shore, tended to side with the French, who appeared to understand them better than did the English, and who knew better how to manipulate them.

The land of the Seneca, except for a notable band of open meadows toward the north, was heavily overgrown with deciduous and coniferous forest, penetrated only by spidery footpaths. This density of forest made travel by water the preferred option for native and newcomer alike. Until late in the eighteenth century, when sailing vessels first began to ply the waters of the upper lakes, such commerce as there was moved along the shoreline of present-day Erie County entirely by bateaux—flat-bottomed open boats driven by men with oars, aided by sail when possible. Bound for Detroit and points further west, freight consisted of military supplies, pork and salt, goods to be traded with western Indians, and, on the return trip, fish and furs.

Following the colonies' successful war for independence from Britain, attention was turned inward, to the land's aboriginal peoples. In a series of duplicitous actions that would be a foretaste of how the new nation would deal with tribes further west, the land was stolen from its original inhabitants. Treaties were signed guaranteeing protection of territory, but the native peoples of New York state could not withstand the pressure of men like Robert Morris, bankroller of the American Revolution, who in 1797 had helped a group of Dutch bankers extinguish Indian title to territory guaranteed them only three years previous by the Treaty of Canandaigua. The Dutch bankers (whose proxies in North America were known unofficially as the Holland Land Company) proceeded to sell the land to a trickle of settlers that they expected to become a flood.

In 1797, following a circus-like treaty-signing at Big Tree, near Geneseo, the Holland Land Company (headquartered in Philadelphia) immediately began to ramp up its western New York operation. The first step was the hiring of surveyors. Joseph Ellicott, who had recently assisted his elder brother Andrew, Surveyor-General of the United States, in staking out a site along the Potomac for a new national capital, was hired as chief surveyor, and, a little later, as agent in charge of land sales. In the spring of 1798, with 150 men weighted down with axes, chains, compasses, theodolites, flags, and muskets, Ellicott and 11 other surveyors plunged into the woods to begin staking out ranges and townships across this vast tract.

The very first order of business for these crews, however, was to be road improvement. The New York state legislature had recently authorized the laying out of a state road from Conewagus (present-day Avon) to Buffalo Creek and another to Lewiston, and the Holland Land Company, whose future could only be brightened by such improved corridors, contributed $5,000 to the enterprise. The road to Buffalo Creek, completed in 1798 and made wide enough for the two-way passage of wagons, ran from Avon through Batavia and along the north shore of Tonawanda Creek to the Tonawanda Indian village. From there it ran over the future site of Akron, through Clarence Hollow and Williamsville, to Cold Spring, afterward following the line of present-day Main Street to Buffalo Creek. Other roads were also improved at this time.

By the winter of 1800, ranges and townships had been laid out, and by 1801 the first tracts were made available for sale. Ellicott would initially set up his land office along the Genesee Road in Clarence Hollow, but soon moved it to Batavia, still beside the increasingly busy route from New England and the Hudson Valley to the west.

Arrangements varied, but land was generally offered at two to three dollars an acre, with 10% down. Since it was not normally the wealthy who ventured into an unknown and forbidding wilderness, but the dispossessed and dreamers, many, not surprisingly, could not afford the down payment. Many of those who could afford it, however—faced as they were with the daunting task of turning the fruit of wilderness agriculture into hard cash—would not be able to keep up payments. Some would see salvation in the company's offer of special terms for a man who would forgo farming to open a log tavern or inn along the new roads. (The Company made land available for this purpose at ten-mile intervals.) Selling liquor, then as now, was a dependable source of income, and more than one erstwhile farmer became prosperous by choosing this path.

The Company's terms and the widespread inability of settlers to pay turned out to be a serious and ongoing problem for the Company and its officers, and feelings against the Company ran high.

With local tribes now relegated to reservations at Buffalo Creek, Tonawanda Creek, Cattaraugus Creek, and Allegany, the land was open. A tide of settlers moved

# The Niagara Frontier

through Batavia and Clarence Hollow, surging on to Williamsville, Cold Spring, and the newly surveyed village of Buffalo, just north of the Buffalo Creek reservation. Pressure was successfully applied to the Senecas to yield their land at the creek's mouth for village access to creek and lake. By 1806, the village could boast 16 dwellings. Ellicott's campaign to name it New Amsterdam was a flop. Villagers insisted upon "Buffaloe," or "Buffalow," in a tug-of-war that soon reached equilibrium in "Buffalo."

Even after convincing the Senecas to give up their land on the north side of Buffalo Creek near the lake, the village from the beginning was hampered by difficult lake access. A sand bar that insisted upon forming across the mouth of Buffalo Creek made entry to the waterway from the lake impossible except for the shallowest-draft—and therefore the smallest—vessels. The village of Black Rock, tucked behind an island in the Niagara River just north of Buffalo and having good access to both river and lake, was the chief lake port in western New York and its citizens were happy to see it stay that way.

Less than ten years after the Purchase had been opened to settlement, talk was heard not only about opening Buffalo Creek somehow to commercial navigation, but, more grandly, about constructing a canal from the Hudson River to Lake Erie, avoiding the equal anguishes of bottomless mud roads (for overland traffic) and the long portage around Niagara Falls (for waterborne traffic). The second war with Britain, however, with its grave consequences for the state and the burgeoning village, would force postponement of such a project for several years.

As the floodgates of migration opened, a percentage of hardy spirits did not stop at Clarence Hollow, Williamsville, or Buffalo, but pushed even further westward along the heavily forested lake shore, or into the wilderness of Erie or Willink, south and east of Buffalo. Settlers who went beyond Buffalo to claim newly purchased tracts, however, faced a life of punishing and relentless toil. Moving out from Buffalo, as the Bennetts would soon do themselves, pushing or helping pull their horse- or ox-drawn wagons through deep lake sand or bottomless mud, they found little to cheer them upon arrival except an awareness of proprietorship—proprietorship, that is, if they could make enough money to keep up their payments.

The new arrivals hacked out small clearings that, in the first winter of occupancy, could host only a stump-surrounded single-windowed log hut. Since land had to be cleared and shelter erected quickly, log walls were frequently left bark-covered, only later to be peeled, and the cabin perhaps floored with puncheons or split logs. Furniture was as primitive as the huts, with a chair or two found only in "upper-class" huts. Bedsteads were rare. A well-off family might have a bed cord strung up on a pole framework, but many made do with the "Holland Purchase bedstead"—long strips of bark strung together in lieu of bed cord.

Some of these huts, if near a local road, might be turned into a tavern or inn, as hopeful farmers came to see that relieving passersby of ready cash with an offer of food, shelter, or liquor was easier than making corn grow amidst tree stumps. Since tree stumps had eventually to be burned, however, the supply of wood ash was plentiful, and many settlers turned to leaching hardwood ashes, boiling the resulting lye solution for its salts, and selling these "black salts" to be further refined at one of the new asheries springing up throughout the Purchase.[7] Wolves were a constant threat to livestock, and many a settler learned to make a living hunting wolves for bounty, which ranged from five dollars in the village of Buffalo to as much as $90 in some outlying towns. Some

---

[7] The lye solution was mixed by the householder with waste cooking grease (animal fat) to make soap, and the potash, the residue of boiling the solution, was used in glassmaking as a flux to lower the melting point of silica. The potash residue could also be baked to make a more refined product called pearlash, which was used and even exported for soap and glass manufacture. Unprocessed ash was used as fertilizer.

# The Niagara Frontier

hunters, it was said, were careful never to kill old she-wolves, since to do so would eventually put an end to a system that ensured them a steady income.

Early settlers lived under the most primitive conditions. More likely to arrive behind a team of oxen than horses (since oxen were relatively inexpensive, hardier than horses, and considered more readily convertible to food), the settler had to build a dwelling before winter. Once the home, a split-rail fence, and an outbuilding or two had been constructed, these "farms" for years after remained covered with interlaced fallen tree trunks, tree branches, and piles of split logs, squared timbers, planks, and shingles. The amount of work to be done was immense. Everything needed for daily life had to be made at home, and nearly everything by hand. Sugar (from the sugar maple) was abundant, but tea and coffee were scarce. Money was extremely scarce. Even after produce was raised there was almost no market, except during the war. Produce frequently had to be hauled as far as Batavia for sale, or to points further east. If it withstood the rigors of forest "highway" transport, the mere cost of making such a trip usually consumed most of the profit.

The construction of gristmills, where corn could be ground into flour, required capital and a dependable water supply for power. For these reasons, gristmills were slow to appear. At the end of 1805, there was not one in the county south of Clarence Hollow. Thus even if a successful crop of corn could be raised in a forest clearing, there remained the extreme difficulty of getting it ground. But without an accessible mill, the pioneers, as usual, made do. A fire would be built atop a stump, and a hollow burned out and scraped clean, then burned and scraped clean again and again until a rude wooden mortar the size of a half-bushel had been hewed out of the stump. In this primitive container, corn would be pounded and reduced to coarse grain with the end of a log, spring-rigged to a neighboring sapling.

# Joseph Bennett

Less capital-intensive were sawmills, although they still required dependable streamflow. If the lack of grist-mills hampered the development of agriculture, the relative lack of sawmills ensured the absence of frame houses in the Purchase for some years.

Whoever could afford to build an actual store—a building of any kind where calico, tea, nails, molasses, ribbons, and salt could be sold for cash—would virtually ensure the development of a settlement on that spot, not to mention a decent living for family and descendants.

In 1812 and 1813 the war with Britain intruded heavily into the lives of Niagara County settlers. Apart from action on the high seas, much of the war was fought along Niagara County waterways—Lake Erie and the Niagara River. Aaron Salisbury, who would meet the Bennetts along the beach in November 1820, and who would become a lifelong friend and mentor of Joseph Bennett, had spent the war years along the lake shore, having lived just west of Sturgeon Point since 1809. During the summer of 1812, with war having recently been declared against Britain, enemy raids were becoming common along the shores of present-day Angola-on-the-Lake, Derby, and Hamburg. From the woods along the low cliffs south of the Eighteen-Mile Creek mouth, the settlers could observe British movements on the lake. During that summer the 26-year-old Salisbury had given rise to a legend by single-handedly driving off a British raiding party sent on a foraging expedition from the 17-gun *HMS Queen Charlotte*, at that time the largest British warship on the lake, riding at anchor off Sturgeon Point. From his place of concealment, he fired on the landing party until they clambered back into their boat and pulled for their ship. He then ran through the woods along the shore to fire on them again near the mouth of Eighteen-Mile Creek, where he had rightly guessed that a new landing would be attempted. The British party, possibly convinced that they faced a regiment, gave up their attempt to land and sailed on down the lake. Following Perry's victory at Presque Isle the following year, British lake forces caused little further trouble.

In December 1813, as the British were advancing upon Buffalo, many residents of the lakeshore area (recently erected as the Town of Eden) hastened to the ultimately unsuccessful defense of the village. Major William Dudley, the town's first schoolmaster, closed up his school to serve, and was killed there. Most able-bodied males were given rank and some training, Aaron Salisbury himself serving as lieutenant of militia.

Following the war, settlers arrived in increasing numbers, and the area around Lake Erie's eastern tip began to undergo an astonishing metamorphosis. In 1817 a turnpike was completed from Albany to Buffalo, and in that same year, plans were drawn up for the longed-for canal across the state. Forest was being inexorably swept away and the presence of every new gristmill, sawmill, or store was taken as a sure sign of a ratcheting-up toward civilization. The Town of Eden, of which modern Evans was then a part, was no exception to this progress. In 1815 and 1816, a sawmill and gristmill were established along Big Sister Creek at Wright's Mills (present-day Evans Center). A post office was erected on the lake shore, soon to be matched by post offices at East Evans (present-day Jerusalem Corners) and Pontiac. The signs of civilization were becoming unmistakable: 1820 saw the inauguration of daily mail service between Buffalo and Albany, and 1821 the coming of young George Sweetland, the town's first physician. On March 16, 1821, following the Bennetts' arrival, a new town named Evans was carved largely out of Eden. (The town was named after Joseph Ellicott's nephew—accounting clerk of the Holland Land Company, New York State senator, later congressman and Holland Land Company agent—David Ellicott Evans.) Two weeks and three days later a new county named Erie was split out of Niagara County.

# Joseph Bennett

In 1820, when the Bennetts came to Williamsville from Union Springs, the population of Niagara County was 23,313, of which 15,668 were in today's Erie County.

♣

On one of those blustery November days in 1820, marked by the crash and roll of waves against the beach, the whistling wind, and the sharp drop in temperature that heralded winter, Aaron Salisbury and others of the young settlement of Eden took it upon themselves to convince the Bennetts to go no farther, but to stay with them, to help build this promising town. They even told of a vacant log house (possibly the house in which they were presently sheltering) with 15 cleared acres that was available for the taking. The restless but sensible Samuel was listening, the Western Reserve moving inexorably out of range of his mind.

"My father concluded to stay," wrote Joseph, "fitted up the old log house, took a tavern license, and commenced keeping a log house hotel, about on a par with others." But the undoubtedly happy young man was about to make an even more pleasing discovery:

> I think it was the third day after our coming here, I took my skates and went out looking for ice. I soon found the mouth of the Big Sister Creek. Upon examination found the ice strong and looked like good skating. Putting on my skates started up the creek. About half a mile up, came to a bend around a *beautiful* flat, thought I never saw a more beautiful spot, went back and reported.

Joseph would begin to frequent this beautiful spot. In ten years he would own it, raise a family there, and dwell on it virtually for the remainder of the century.

# 3

# *YOUNG MAN IN EVANS*

The vacant log house on the Lake Erie shore, with its 15 acres of cleared land, turned out to have been unused for some time. Its latest owner, one John Lay, had never made an appearance to claim it, and the family needed little convincing to move in and set up a promising business. Yet another watering-hole would now be available to beach travelers.

Over the winter, under the tutelage of James Peters, 17-year-old Joseph attended school two miles away at Jerusalem Corners, and the following summer helped his father on a farm that Samuel was working on shares. But during the spring he had begun to contract fishing fever, and felt the growing need of a boat to assuage it. He had watched how the family's neighbors made boats for themselves, and commenced to make one for his own use. Two of his brothers, 14-year-old Alonzo and 10-year-old Samuel, helped him.

"We . . . cut down a very large beautiful tree," he recounted,

worked away until a large and pretty nice canoe came out, about 20 feet long. It was drawn to the mouth of the creek, and the following arrangements made:

First a spear, then arrangements for a light, by nailing a platform 3-1/2 feet square across the canoe 3 or 4 feet forward of midship, then putting a covering

41

of clay mortar over the platform sufficiently thick to secure from fire.

The boys one evening slid their fire-bearing, hand-made craft into Big Sister Creek, jumped in, and miraculously avoided both capsize and conflagration in the top-heavy vessel. "I being the eldest of the three," wrote Joseph, "took my place in the bow, as chief spearman. Fish were very plenty."

He continued:

> The big fire on the canoe, dazzled the eyes of the fish and made it light as day for us. I soon saw a large fish at the bottom of the creek, the water at least 4 feet deep. (The fish I wanted very much.) But there was a long limb or root of a tree over 4 feet long, floating just below the surface of the water, between me and the fish. I was at a loss how to act—could not spear the fish without moving the root, and if I moved the root, would surely scare the fish. But must try anyway.

He slipped his spear into the water, moved it slowly down toward the root, and carefully began to prod the root out of the way. "As [my spear] touched the root," he said, "the water flew all over us, the root was a monster muscalonge [sic]!" He was frantic at his loss. "I could only just jump up and down, don't think I swore, but learned a lesson about seeing fish."

Boyish pursuits apart, his talents and leadership potential were becoming obvious to his neighbors, for in the spring of 1821, shortly after the new Town of Evans and County of Erie were erected, 17-year old Joseph was appointed "Town Marshall," with his first assignment to take a census of the new town, which numbered probably 1,000 or less. (One suspects that Aaron Salisbury, increasingly influential in town affairs, had something to do with young Joseph's appointment.)[8] Further respon-

---

[8] Salisbury would eventually serve seven terms as town supervisor and one term in the state assembly. He would be a delegate to the

sibilities were in the offing: the following winter he was hired to teach school at Evans Center, taking over a class of 60 students, many of whom were older than he. ("Must have been an excellent school," he quipped.)

Talk of schools and farm life and the carefree pursuits of children tempts one to imagine a fairly civilized setting for the Bennetts and their neighbors, but the reality was quite otherwise. The town was only a step removed from wilderness. "There was one small brick house," wrote Joseph,

> partly finished, and two or three cheap framed houses (and small) in the "then" Town of Evans. All others were log houses and generally very poor.
>
> The settlers in this county and in fact all over the Holland Purchase have had a hard time. Labored terribly hard and endured an endless amount of privations.
>
> No one would ever have settled here as farmers if the Western Prairies had been in market.

"This, however," he concluded, somewhat prophetically, "is destined to be a rich, and valuable old country, but not until the pioneers, *men and women*, are worked to death. Then it will be a beautiful country."

If any historical "moment" could be said to have marked the end of pioneer times in western New York, it would have been 1821-22. A new county and new towns had been erected, roads were being improved, sawmills and gristmills constructed, and the outlook for commerce in general was brightening. Log huts were beginning to give way to brick and frame homes, settlements were starting to resemble towns, and, for a growing segment of the population, life was becoming less desperate.

---

state constitutional convention of 1846, and would serve as an associate justice of the Court of Common Pleas.

# Joseph Bennett

Despite ongoing improvements to local roads, however, transportation remained a major obstacle to trade and development. ("*Such roads, O such roads*," said Joseph, "after the winter breaks up.") The land was only a generation removed from wilderness, and overland travel still required a generous degree of fortitude. "Roads" in Erie County, passable, at least, for the three dry-weather months, were quite otherwise for the remainder of the year. (The worst road in the county, it was said, was the "Four-Mile Woods," today's Four-Mile Level Road between Irving and Gowanda, reputed to have absolutely no bottom.) Big stagecoaches bowled along fairly easily during summer, but woe to the unlucky coach traveler in spring or fall. Half the time would be spent in trudging along next to the conveyance instead of riding in it, with a significant portion of that time spent in helping the horses to extract the vehicle from the omnipresent, sucking mud.

Clearly something had to be done to improve transportation, and it was obvious that the best chance for immediate improvement lay in the direction of water. As mentioned previously, there had been talk before the war of constructing a canal from the Hudson River to Lake Erie, promising to make possible a relatively comfortable and rapid trip from New York City to the upper Great Lakes. For the duration of the war this idea was dropped, but immediately after the war it was revived. Activist politician De Witt Clinton, a man who would build an impressive political resume (mayor of New York City, state assemblyman and senator, lieutenant governor, U.S. senator, presidential candidate, two-time governor, and New York canal commissioner), was its strongest supporter. By 1815, in fact, the public, thoroughly sick of the roads of the day, was behind the plan, and in April of that year a bill passed the New York state assembly authorizing immediate commencement of work. A route was soon surveyed from Buffalo to the Genesee River, and by July 1817 actual construction was under way on the Rome-Utica section.

# Young Man in Evans

Despite this brisk and businesslike beginning, for the next several years of construction it remained undecided exactly where the canal's western terminus would be. Would it be Buffalo exactly, or neighboring Black Rock? The latter initially held the stronger hand, because it was widely known that entry into Buffalo Creek from Lake Erie by any but the smallest craft was impossible. As mentioned earlier, the presence of a sandbar at the mouth of the creek restricted travel into the creek to shallow-draft vessels, incapable of carrying any serious tonnage.

Since no one seemed willing or able to undertake removal of the sandbar, in 1820 Judge Samuel Wilkeson took over the job himself, and by 1822, against great odds and using inventive methods, he and his crew had made it possible for a large steamship to enter and leave the creek safely. The efforts of Judge Wilkeson opened the future for Buffalo as a major commercial hub. By the summer of 1823 it had been decided to establish the canal's western terminus at Buffalo, and in August of that year, the first spadeful of earth was turned to create the new Port of Buffalo in the sheltered reaches of lower Buffalo Creek. Still left to be accomplished was the construction (at a place that became known as Lockport) of five closely spaced and ingenious double locks to lift westbound boat traffic up the 65-foot-high Niagara escarpment and to ease eastbound traffic down it.

Eighteen-year-old Joseph Bennett saw an employment opportunity here and moved to grasp it. "In the summer of 1822," he wrote, "I was in Lock Port a short time working on the canal." Following this first stint of what would become many years in heavy construction, he came back to his parents' home and stayed with them during the winter of 1822-23. He would return to Lockport the following spring, but in between he would enjoy the winter at home.

"During the winter," he wrote,

# Joseph Bennett

I had no particular employment. Spent a large proportion of my time breaking colts, and riding around in a jumper. Cutters were not known in this community. A jumper is a cheap made one horse concern, made as follows. We get two green poles, or saplings about 12 feet long or less, 2-1/2 inches through at the but [sic], shave out a notch in each pole commencing 4-1/2 feet from the but end, shave enough out, to enable the pole to bend easily. Now you have the runners and shafts combined, now bore two inch holes in each runner where the beams should be, drive in a strong pin in each hole, which forms the knees of the jumper, put the two beams onto these pins and you have the carriage, ready to receive a dry goods box or crate to ride in.

He could, he declared, make a jumper in three hours.

Despite the roads being "entirely new and full of stumps," and despite frequent conveyance upsets, Joseph spent his time during the winter giving "the ladies" of Evans sleigh rides. While snow to some extent neutralized the effect of the stumps and made the roads passable, the very best wintertime avenues were on lake ice, which was used even by stagecoaches. "As soon as the ice is strong enough on the lake," he wrote, ". . . the travel is nearly all upon the ice,"

and every inn keeper makes a road from his house to the track on the lake.

Much work is often done to fix the road on the ice. Ice *shoves* are leveled, little hemlock trees or *tops* are stuck into the ice every thirty or forty rods to mark the road and guide travelers in snow storms or night.

Occasional accidents happen. Mr. Barr of Cataraugus [sic] Creek lost a stage team of 4 fine horses. They were traveling at a fine gait, when the leaders broke through. The wheel horses plunged in, and drove the leaders under the ice. The stage then drove the wheel horses under. Passengers just barely saved, after receiving a very unpleasant bath.

# Young Man in Evans

"One other span of horses lost," he added, "both this winter."

Shortly after the appearance of spring blossoms in 1823, he returned to Lockport, this time to remain there for the entire summer and autumn as clerk and foreman for a Town of Evans contractor: Dibble, Olmstead and Landon. Orange Hezekiah ("O.H.") Dibble, a man with a number of business interests and already credited with an invention that speeded up the excavation of rock at Lockport, had arrived in Evans as a young man in 1811. Dibble, in his mid-thirties at the time, would be an important influence in young Bennett's life.

Twenty-year-old Joseph, doubtless tanned and fit from his months of heavy outdoor work in Lockport, spent the following winter at home with his family, again occupying himself with giving sleigh rides to the young ladies, with the same rollicking upsets in snowdrifts due to the condition of the roads. "No particular harm done," he said.

During this winter he and his friends came up with an idea for winter fun that was a little out of the ordinary. To carry it out, five yoke of oxen were produced by Joseph and three of his friends, Ira Ayer, James Reed, and "young Bates." Also produced was a quart of whiskey, to which was added a quart of molasses to make a large jug of blackstrap. A bag with some "johnnycake and dryed [sic] beef" was packed up, whether to ward off the effects of the cold or the blackstrap is not clear. A driver, one Harlow Rowley, was hired for the night. Rowley would not be allowed to ride, but would be required to walk with the oxen all night on the planned eight-mile round trip. His compensation would be fifty cents and unlimited blackstrap access.

"All arrangements being made," wrote Joseph, "we now ordered the driver to bring up the carriage." The harnessed oxen, forming a line nearly fifty feet long, were now brought to the door and the sled box filled with straw. There were no seats. Piling into the box with the jug, their provisions, and a five-foot long tin boat-horn, the revelers gave orders to move on. "Away we went," said Joseph, "at the rate of 3 miles to the hour." The cold was intense, he recalled, but, burrowed into the straw, all were "comfortable and happy."

Driving west from today's Roat Acres area along the stump-filled lakeshore road, they stopped first at the house of town supervisor James Aldrich, near present-day Bennett Beach. One suspects that their stops were decided on the basis of whether young females were at home. They took "peaceable possession" of the Aldrich family home, remembered Joseph, the family seeming to "enter into the spirit" of the festivities. The family was reluctant, however, to enter completely into that spirit. "Had to almost force them to drink out of the jug," wrote Joseph, "but they did."

Heading back to their "sleigh" and their doubtless shivering driver, they moved on to the house of O.H. Dibble, Joseph's employer of the previous summer. "Mr. Dibble was not in the house but Mrs. Dibble entered into the spirit."

> On we went. The snow being very deep, our driver became very tired and begged to ride. Would not have him in the sleigh with us but consented to let him ride astride the sled tongue. The passengers took turns at blowing the horn.

The merrymakers' next stop was at Whiting Cash's, near Point Breeze. "At all our stopping places they had large fires," recalled Joseph. "They were also very pleasant at this place, as at others." But at Cash's a serious accident befell the group: someone knocked over the jug of blackstrap. Ira Ayer drew cleanup duty, but the floor was reportedly already too dirty, pre-spill, for this operation to succeed. (The Cash family having a number of young children in a log cabin, wrote Joseph, the floor was not "in perfect order.") At 10 PM they moved on to "old Mr. Cash's," where they found that the "2 Misses

# Young Man in Evans

Cash" had turned in.[9]  Upon the visitors' "strong and urgent requests," the Misses Cash got up to join in the revelry. "We had a nice time," wrote Joseph, "proved ourselves liberal with our refreshments."

Just after midnight, they turned their patient oxen homeward, four miles through the snowy darkness, arriving home nearly two hours later.

Before winter's chill surrendered its hold that year, Joseph, who had learned to love sailing in his years on Cayuga Lake, and who now had some change in his pocket from the previous summer's canal work, felt the growing call of the water. "Sometime during this winter (1824)," he wrote, "I bought a small vessel, the sloop *Ohio* from a man by the name of Brown of Ashtabula, Ohio."

> The sloop was lying in Buffalo Creek, at the foot of Main street. She was a small vessel of not more than 25 ton burden. Vessels on the lake are all small. Over 50 tons burden is considered too large for the trade, average size between 30 and 40 tons. There was one vessel, schooner 150 tons burden, the *Michigan*, she not profitable, freight all up the lake, nothing down. There is one steamer on the lakes, the *Superior*.[10]

In mid-April 1824 20-year old Joseph went to Buffalo, put up at a boarding house, and started looking around the waterfront for a sailor to help handle his new vessel, with which he intended to enter the lake trade. He found and hired a small, wiry Scotsman by the name of John Love, a man who claimed to have been at sea

---

[9] By "old Mr. Cash," Joseph is presumably referring to William Cash, who was just over 60 at the time.

[10] In 1827 the unprofitable *Michigan* would be disposed of by sending it, adorned with effigies of General Andrew Jackson and other dignitaries, and—unpleasantly, to us—"crewed" by captive animals (three bears, a penned bison, two foxes, a dog, a cat, a raccoon, and four geese), over the Horseshoe Falls. The *Superior* was the second steamship built in western New York. Converted back to a full-rigged sailing vessel in 1834, it was wrecked on Lake Michigan in October 1843.

since running away from home at the age of 10. Love told young Bennett that he had served aboard the U.S. frigate *Constitution* in its famous actions against the *HMS Guerriere* and *HMS Java* during the past war. Joseph took him aboard gladly, and was pleased to find that he was indeed an excellent seaman.

"Commenced fitting out the sloop," he wrote, "had her fitted out in good condition the 10th of May. As soon as the ice was out of the lake we sailed with a small cargo for Dunkirk and Portland."[11]

This first of Joseph's trips on the *Ohio* was to prove memorable.

> After discharging our freight took in part of a load of Pot. [potash] and Pearl Ash and a family, man, wife and children, for Buffalo. We sailed from Portland, one evening, about sundown, with a very heavy south wind. About 11 o'clock, just off Dunkirk a terrible gale struck us. We saw it coming, just had time to take in our main sail, were running under light canvas. The jib went, like a piece of brown paper. For a short time we scud before the wind. About one o'clock we laid the vessel to and lashed ourselves to the quarter rail. John Love lashed by the side of me. The sea very high and washed us severely. The little vessel behaved beautifully.

The passengers had remained in the sloop's small cabin throughout.

"They were terribly frightened," said Joseph,

> and not without cause or reason. It was really a frightful time. At daylight were about fifteen miles out of Buffalo. We then set the flying jib and wore away before the wind, it blowing right into Buffalo. When we arrived in a short time all right, our little vessel proved to be a splendid sea craft.

Being responsible for the now potentially damaged cargo, Joseph, prior to "breaking bulk," entered a protest

---

[11] Portland Harbor is present-day Barcelona.

# Young Man in Evans

before Stephen G. Austin, Justice of the Peace and Notary Public, describing the circumstances over which he had had no control. But, to his relief, "after opening the hatches, found the cargo all right, no damage done."

♣

Shipmates on small vessels get to know each other sooner rather than later, and Joseph and his crewman Love were soon comfortable with one another. One day in June, Love, who spent his summers on the lake and his winters on peddling tours around the county, lodging with a family in North Boston, told Joseph that he had three $25 notes outstanding against the family with whom he stayed—the Thayers. Payment was due on November 1, he said, but—likely because of the penurious condition in which his hosts lived—he was afraid he would not collect. He asked young Bennett, who appeared to know his way around a courthouse, to sue the Thayers for him and then turn the money over to him once judgment had been secured.

The Thayers consisted of Israel Thayer and his three sons, Nelson, Israel Jr., and Isaac. The elder two, Nelson and Israel, were in their early twenties, and Isaac barely out of his teens. The two eldest were married, and presumably did not live with their father and younger brother. Love appears to have resided with Israel Sr. and Isaac, although not exclusively. The Thayer boys had a reputation for drunkenness, violence, and general unorthodoxy. In addition to dressing oddly, they took pride in needling their more conservative neighbors by referring to one of their oxen as God Almighty and the other as Jesus Christ. In reference to the young Thayers, one contemporary judged that "human life would not be of much value in their hands."

Being an industrious man, Love usually had money, and he had loaned $75 of it to the Thayers. He was now asking Joseph to help ensure that the debt would be collected.

# Joseph Bennett

I very inocently [sic] consented. Took summons of Esqr. S.G. Austin. On the return day the Thayers came into court and said that, Love promised to wait until the first of November and that they were making calculations to pay at that time without fail. I then said to them, Confess judgement and give bail for stay of execution to the first of November, and I will wait, which they did. It was now all safe, and I was pleased with the arrangement. I came from the court room to the vessel, and reported to Love, what I had done, expecting he also would be pleased, but instead, was very angry. I then discovered the wickedness of the man.

Bennett's eyes had been opened. He now saw Love to be a mean, grasping fellow, bent on forcing collection and taking possession of what little property the Thayers owned. Unhappy with this turn of events, he discharged his new hand a few days later.

During the remainder of the summer, Bennett, with a fresh crew, continued in the lake trade, making short and frequent trips as far west as Erie. He was busy and successful, hopeful of an early payoff on the debt on his vessel. "We had a nice little trade at Cataraugus [sic] Creek," he noted. "Our business was along shore business, during the summers pleasant weather, would land almost any where to discharge or take goods." He dealt with Townsend and Coit, the only forwarding merchants in Buffalo. He predicted that because of the rapid increase in lake trade, large wharfs and storehouses would be erected in Buffalo, and the tonnage carried on boats like his would increase dramatically. He fairly bubbled over with his vision for the future: "The Western country being developed, Erie Canal soon finished, Buffalo harbor being enlarged, every man walking erect and stately, with his hat turned up in front."

Business was so good that he tried to keep it going into November, a month when any turn of meteorological events is possible on Lake Erie. "The first week in November," he recalled,

> I shipped a lot of goods for Cataraugus [*sic*], consigned to Ralph Plumb.[12] We sailed from Buffalo in the morning, the weather and wind being unfavorable. We run into Dibble's Bay and came to anchor.

Bennett had anchored in the lee of the point near present-day Central Avenue, east of Point Breeze, to wait for better sailing conditions and to spend the night at his parents' home, about a mile away near the mouth of Little Sister Creek. He continued:

> That night the wind changed from south west to north west and blew a gale. I was on shore and at my father's house . . . when the squall struck. I immediately started on foot, and ran, to the shore opposite the vessel, and signaled the men to come on shore for me, and they nearly swamped in getting shore. After ever so many trials found it impossible to get through the surf, a tremendous sea coming square in, all we could do was to watch the vessel from shore, no one on board. My only fear was that she would strike bottom, and of course if she did, that would end her. When darkness came on, all went to my father's one mile away for supper, and to wait events.

> About midnight, the wind began to lull. We took a lantern, and all started, for the vessel along the lake shore. When within about 100 rods of being opposite the vessel, found some apples washed ashore, which I knew came from the cabin of the vessel. I knew then she was down . . . After the sea calmed down a little, we went off to the vessel and found her sunk.

Next day, enlisting the help of friends and neighbors, the young captain hoisted out the freight—groceries, other perishables, dry goods—and brought it ashore for sorting and drying. The owner of the cargo, Ralph Plumb,

---

12 Ralph Plumb was a Gowanda merchant.

was notified, and immediately sent men overland to haul it away—"much of it in damaged condition."

"After relieving the vessel of freight," explained Bennett, "we rigged a purchase, got her onto ways, and hauled her out."

Going down in the trough of heavy seas, the vessel had struck bottom hard, explained Bennett, "unshiped [sic] her rudder," which stuck fast in the lake bottom, then had come down hard atop the rudder head, driving a hole in the vessel's quarter.

Ralph Plumb had lost his cargo; his only recourse was to sue the young transporter for damages.

"Sometime during the month of November," wrote Joseph,

> I was taken on a warrant to Gowanda, before Squire Pitcher and judgements were obtained against me for $300.00. I came home from Gowanda as you may well suppose entirely crushed, just 21 years of age and liable any day to be sent to debtors jail.

Deeply in debt now, he gave up the idea of being a lake trader, sold the sloop the following spring, and paid off most of his debts. His last foray into lake trading would be the following summer, when he would help his friends the Cashes fit out a small vessel for carrying lumber, and assist them in getting it out onto the lake for its first trip.

♣

By November, the Thayers' had apparently made good on repayment of their debt, because Love had moved in again with them, evidently not noticing, or not choosing to notice, the men's changed attitude toward him.

One cold day in early December 1824, the Thayers slaughtered their hogs at the house of young Israel, whose wife had been "sent away." Love had been invited to join them, although he was not expected to participate in the butchering. As darkness fell, having no better place to work, Nelson and Isaac dragged the bloody hog carcasses into the small, low, log house to cut them up in the warmth of a roaring fire. They worked on the hogs at the far end of the room, away from the fire, while Love sat in a fireside chair, his back to the hog operation. He was wearing the Navy pea jacket that he had worn during the war, and which Joseph himself had occasionally worn during night watches on the lake. About 8 PM, the muzzle of a rifle was eased through one of the darkened window openings, and Love was shot through the head.

Bennett gives the version he had later heard of what happened after young Israel pulled the trigger.

> Love . . . did not stir from his position. One of the boys behind him, thinking he was not hit with the bullet, struck him with the ax he was using, cutting meat. Love fell from the chair dead . . . The three young men with their father, all implicated alike, took the dead body, buried it in a ravine some distance from the house, it being up on the hills in the Town of Boston.
>
> In a day or two they removed the body to Chestnut ridge.

During subsequent weeks, the Thayers' neighbors could not help but notice that the family was living better than it had ever lived before. It was especially noticeable at the Christmas Day turkey shoot, where local marksmen usually economized on ammunition, which cost six pence a shot. The Thayers on this occasion kept up a steady fire, seeming not to care if they hit or missed, and tossed their coins out with abandon for the purchase of ammunition. People also noticed that they seemed to have a good deal of John Love's personal property, including a fine saddle horse. The murderers were eventually undone when they tried to collect debts owed to Love, claiming that Love, who they said was off peddling somewhere, had empowered them to do so. Since they could produce nothing but a clearly bogus letter of attorney, local authorities soon paid them a visit and pointedly asked where John Love was. By February 1825 Nelson and young Israel had been arrested for murder, and a large-scale search commenced for the body of Love, the Town of Boston magistrate offering a reward of ten dollars for its recovery.

"Almost the entire community turned out," recalled young Bennett, "and searched for the supposed body of Love."

> They examined every conceivable place imaginable, continued the search during the first day and made no discovery. The Thayers [Israel Sr. and Isaac] were with the people all day in the search. At night the old man Thayer asked some of the men, if they had searched on Chestnut ridge. They said no. "Strang [sic] that the old man should speak of Chestnut Ridge." The people took the hint. They went to Chestnut ridge the next morning and found the body of John Love.

Love's decomposed body was discovered lying on its back in a shallow, brush-covered grave, his toes sticking out of the frozen ground. Isaac and his father were arrested immediately.

"The judgements that I obtained against the Thayers, . . ." said Joseph, "proved to be the bone of contention which caused the murder."

"On the same day," he continued,

> in which the murder was committed my father had business in Hamburgh, only 3 or 4 miles from the Thayers, where Love was boarding. And as I owed Love some money, balance due on last summers work on my vessel, I sent it with my father.

> The roads being muddy, and the weather turning cold, the roads became almost impassable. [My father] was intending to reach Love's boarding place at about 8 o'clock, P.M., just about the time of the murder, but was obliged to stop at Hamburgh. It looks rather providential, the money was brot [sic] back.

# Young Man in Evans

While all four Thayers had been taken into custody, evidence against the father was not strong, and only the sons were indicted. In mid-April, the three Thayer sons were tried, convicted of murder, and sentenced to death. Following their conviction, they made a full confession, insisting that their father had had nothing to do with the plan or its execution. They were sentenced to be hanged in June, and were remanded to the old stone jail on Washington Street until then.

Between the Thayers' trial and execution—both events that held the public for miles around in thrall—other, oddly diversionary, events occurred. In early May, the canal section from Buffalo to Tonawanda was filled with water, and the steamer *Superior*, appropriately decked out and loaded with revelers, headed down the Niagara River to swing into the canal through the newly built lock near the mouth of Tonawanda Creek. Met by boats from as far away as Lockport, the *Superior* then proceeded—to the thundering of cannon and the cheering of shoreline crowds—back to Buffalo, where further festivities awaited.

On June 3 occurred a second distraction from the business of a triple execution. It had recently been announced that the Marquis de Lafayette, friend of President Washington and hero of the American Revolution, wished to stop in Buffalo on his way home to France from a tour of the United States. He would come overland from Erie to Dunkirk. He wished to be met by ship at Dunkirk and be taken to Buffalo.

The *Superior* was again decked out in flags and bunting, and, amid preparations for Lafayette's arrival, steamed out to Dunkirk, where the general was brought aboard as planned. The lake that day was wild, however, and its condition prevented the ship from entering its home port on schedule. Following several attempts, the *Superior* eventually succeeded in entering the creek and disembarking its famous passenger. Lafayette, to the oom-pah-pah of the village band and the cheers of its citizens, toured the small village. From a dais in present-day Lafayette Square, he then addressed the assembled throng, which had come from miles around to hear him. The visit concluded with a banquet in Lafayette's honor given at the Eagle Tavern, reputedly the finest hotel on the frontier. The general departed on the following day, stopping at Niagara Falls on his way eastward.

Once the general was out of sight, carpenters began construction of a scaffold on the west side of present-day Niagara Square, and on June 17, the three Thayers, dressed in white caps and shrouds, and preceded by a cart carrying three coffins, were marched from the old stone jail to the scaffold on Court Street.[13] Bystanders noted their self-possession. A band played a slow and plaintive air, while road-clogging crowds conservatively estimated at more than 10,000 pressed forward to witness the awful sight of three brothers being hanged together.

Following a short sermon and prayer, during which the doomed men remained seated atop the scaffold, the prisoners rose, said their farewells to one another, had their arms pinioned, halters placed and adjusted, and took their places on the fatal drop. At 1:45 PM the three were, in the expression of the time, "launched into eternity." Following the execution, Israel Thayer, Sr., was released from custody.

Bennett, feeling a close connection with the events leading up to this day, was part of the crowd. "A revolting sight," was his only comment.

♧

In October 1825, arguably the most portentous month in Buffalo's history, the Erie Canal was opened from New York harbor and the Hudson River to the Port of Buffalo. The population of the village, then about 2,400, would soon explode almost exponentially. On Oc-

---

[13] The date commonly given for this execution is June 7. June 17 is given by Nathaniel Wilgus, a member of a militia company assigned to guard the prisoners, and an eyewitness to the execution.

tober 26, the *Seneca Chief* set off down the new water-way from Buffalo, freighted not only with Gov. De Witt Clinton and many pounds of dignitaries, but also with two barrels of Lake Erie water for ceremonial dumping into New York harbor. It would take until November 4 for the *Chief* to reach New York, its progress slowed somewhat by an orgy of canalside celebration, and its return—the vessel now bearing a keg of Atlantic water—would take until November 23. In an unwitting foreshadowing of the speed of future travel, cannons had been set up along the waterway for the eastward voyage, with the first cannon to be fired in Buffalo on the *Seneca Chief's* departure, and each subsequent cannon to be fired when the cannon to westward was heard. The resulting auditory ripple reached New York harbor in one hour and twenty minutes.

The immediate effect of the canal's opening was not increased trade or lower prices, but an increased influx of people—whether transients or new residents. The canal's packet boats in fact brought more people than goods. Since, however, the number of immigrants and transients far exceeded the capacity of the canal to carry them, stagecoach business also increased accordingly.

Nevertheless, as 1825 rolled into 1826 and 1827 the price of shipping began to drop dramatically, making it possible now for western New York farmers to ship their goods economically to more distant markets, even to Albany and New York. Transit times, in addition to overall costs, were reduced. Even postal rates dropped. Buffalo became the exchange point between east and west, and opportunities for moneymaking multiplied geometrically. Warehouses and lodgings were built, port facilities were expanded, amenities increased. Optimism was contagious as the growing village faced what appeared to be a very bright future indeed.

Personal clocks can run at a different tempo from regional or national clocks. It is always possible to be out of sync with one's environment. Joseph Bennett, having recently lost his livelihood, was not swept up in the region's optimism. "During the winter of 1825 and 26," he wrote,

> am at home at my father's. Time goes off very monotinous [sic], no particular calculations for the future. Thought perhaps I might take a birth [sic] on the lake as mate or something of that kind, not decided.

Since his parents were opposed to his spending further time as a lake sailor, he did not pursue this notion. But his life was about to turn in a useful direction, albeit one unrelated to lake sailing.

In October he had taken the step of initiation into the Masons, whose principal members were the town's new doctor, George Sweetland, Aaron Salisbury, local businessmen William van Duzer and William W. Morsman, and his father. Van Duzer was agent for a stage line owned by O.H. Dibble, for whom young Bennett had recently worked in canal construction at Lockport. In light of the anti-Masonic feeling taking shape in the region at this time, becoming a Mason may have given him some pause, but it also doubtless gave him some stature in the community, and likely opened some doors that might otherwise have remained closed. "One day in the month of May [1826]," he wrote,

> I met Mr. Van Duzer in the street. He stopped me and asked if I would drive stage for him two or three days, that one driver had left and would be very glad if I would drive for a very short time until he could get one. I told him yes I would drive to accommodate until he could get a driver.

While young Bennett filled in as stage driver, the line's astute owner, O.H. Dibble, by now a seasoned canal contractor, was in Pennsylvania sniffing around for canal construction contracts along the Susquehanna River near Harrisburg.

"Some time about the first of July," wrote Joseph,

# Young Man in Evans

Mr. Dibble came home. Had taken 3 or 4 sections of canal to build and was going back as soon as possible to commence work. He sold his stage route and reserved one team and carriage, *that one I was driving*. He proposed my going with him to assist in managing his work, which I gladly consented to do. In less than two weeks, were on our way to Pennsylvania.

Joseph Bennett, who turned 23 on arrival in Pennsylvania, would not see parents or siblings for the next three years. He would be occupied full-time in heavy construction some 300 miles from home.

# 4

# CONSTRUCTING THE FUTURE

Overland travel in the wilds of Pennsylvania was no easier than in New York. Like New York's roads and turnpikes, Pennsylvania's were stump-filled, boulder-strewn morasses that presented a great obstacle to the flow of goods and people and, ultimately, the dissemination of wealth. Prior to the 1820s, waterborne commerce on the generally north-south-lying rivers was possible where depth permitted, but long-distance east-west travel by water was not. Philadelphia and Pittsburgh might well have existed on separate and distant islands.

It was the Appalachian Mountains that presented, as they did along most of the eastern seaboard, a significant barrier to east-west movement. The state of New York was fortunate in having the Mohawk Valley as a passageway through this wall, and, because of this, found it relatively easy to construct a canal between the Hudson River and the Great Lakes. The Commonwealth of Pennsylvania was not so fortunate, with the approximately 2,000-foot-high Allegheny Front, a deeply cleft escarpment angling northeast-southwest across much of the state, forming a virtually impassable barrier to east-west waterborne commerce. Despite the seeming impossibility of carrying on such commerce across this barrier, Pennsylvania's political and business leaders in the 1820s—in order to ensure that the Keystone State would not be left behind by its industrious neighbor to the north—determined to do exactly that: namely, to build an east-west canal system across the entire state.

In April 1825, six months before the opening of New York State's Erie Canal, the Pennsylvania legislature established a Board of Canal Commissioners to oversee construction and maintenance of a state canal system. Top engineers were hired to produce designs and oversee construction, and a small army of laborers was brought in to do the pick and shovel work. Many were immigrants: Chinese, German, Irish. These men, anxious to make their way in a new land, would know hard work, deprivation, and disease, but, as their people had done elsewhere, they would succeed. By the time Pennsylvania's canals had been supplanted by railroads—a short two decades later—these immigrants would have helped construct over 1,300 miles of canals, almost one-quarter of the nation's total canal mileage, and the most extensive canal system of any state.

And the Allegheny Front problem was solved in spectacular fashion: barges and packets, with cargo and passengers, were loaded onto rail cars and carried 36 miles across the mountain on a series of inclined railways, to be placed back in the water on the other side.

♧

On July 4, 1826 (coincidentally the date on which both Thomas Jefferson and John Adams died), construction commenced in the so-called Eastern Division, the state letting contracts for work along the east bank of the Susquehanna between Columbia, some 30 miles downstream of Harrisburg, and Clark's Ferry, about 15 miles upstream of the city. It was during this month, while Joseph Bennett was filling in as stage driver in western New York, that O.H. Dibble was in Harrisburg bidding on the work.

Dibble was soon awarded contracts for the construction of several sections of canal across a small rocky and steep-hilled peninsula where the river curls sharply around the municipalities of Reed and Middle Paxton in Dauphin County, eight miles upstream of Harrisburg. He and several other contractors would be responsible for constructing the guard lock at Peters Mountain, where westbound canal traffic would enter the river and eastbound traffic would leave it; four lift locks south of the mountain; and an aqueduct over Clark's Creek. On award of the contracts, he hastened home to settle his business affairs, including selling his stage route, hired young Bennett and another Evans man, Isaiah Gray, as construction managers, and, driving his one remaining coach and team, returned to Pennsylvania. It was early August 1826. The area where they would spend the next three years was known as Red Hill.

"We found a very nice rich country," recalled Joseph of his arrival at Red Hill, "and all Germans and honest, well to do farmers. They were not very favorably inclined toward us at first but after a while we gained their entire confidence."

They had plenty of reasons, he noted, to dislike "Yankees," a label that embraced New Yorkers as well as New Englanders. "In the spring freshets," he said,

> there are *hundreds of men.* "Raft men and Ark men" go down the river with rafts of lumb[er] and arks of coal, and plaster. They return home, up the river, in squads, on foot. And a hard lot of men they are. Then there are the Yankee clock pedlers [*sic*] and lightning rod men. On the whole, the Germans have formed a dislike to the Yankees. But the public works are introducing all classes and nationalities of men. Prejudice is just beginning to subside. Against us, it is all gone. I never lived among a better people.

After a quick trip to Harrisburg to see his father's younger brother Seymour, who—only about ten years older than Joseph—lived there with his family, Bennett set to work, helping to purchase materials and tools and hire laborers. The Evans men, who would be engaged mostly in rock excavation, were inundated with job applicants, largely Germans and Irishmen. Outside his regular working hours, which were dawn until dark, Bennett was entrusted with the books. "I kept the books," he said,

> and was on the works every day, done all the writing nights and Sundays. Performed the work of two men, all that fall and winter. Trusting entirely upon Mr. Dibble's liberality for the amount of my salary. Wages very low, paid our men fifty cents per day, if we boarded them, and seventy-five cents, if they boarded themselves.

In summer the men began work at dawn and took a half-hour break for breakfast at 7:30 AM, then worked until nightfall, with an hour off for dinner. In winter, breakfast was before daylight, and the men set to work as soon as Bennett could see to call the roll.

Young Bennett spent his free time with the local Germans, including attendance at "apple butter boilings" and "Straus dances" (a game involving a pile of trinkets called a Straus). But once the leaves of 1826 had been shed, he would meet someone who would take his mind off such entertainments. "The middle of November," he wrote,

> Mrs. Dibble [the former Jane Roat] came to Pennsylvania by the way of New York City and New Jersey, and brought her sister Mary Roat from New Jersey. The first time I saw Mary she was sitting in the family circle around the fire, in the family sitting room at their boarding house. As I came into the room Mary arrose [sic] and I was introduced to her. A girl, 18 years old, small in stature, fine figure, well developed, beautiful black, fine, soft, glossy hair. Black, pleasant, intelligent eyes, and quick active, sprightly movement.

The Roat sisters were the daughters of Michael and Margaret Roat of Englishtown, New Jersey. Jane Roat Dibble was at this time about 30. It is unclear how she had met O.H. Dibble.

# Constructing the Future

His first impression was that Mary was "an *excellent girl*." And if he had as yet no premonition that she would one day be his wife, he soon received a prophecy in this vein.

> One day I had a man cutting up beef and packing in an out house, a very excentric [*sic*] mulatto. As I stood there, he turned and looked at me for half a minute. Then quietly said, you will be married within the year, and be in the way of making money.

Bennett kept the books in the evening and on weekends, and found time to go out socially with Mary, but during the day he occupied himself with blasting. "Our work," he explained,

> was heavy rock work, along the eastern bank of the Susquehanna River. There was a large amount of blasting of which I took special charge. One man in January [1827] had his eyes destroyed by a blast. I made some pretty heavy sand blasts with from two to three kegs of powder to a blast of 25 lbs. each.

As in Union Springs ten years before, when the teen-age Bennett had nearly blown up not only himself but also his employers' store, black powder in 1827 was a fact of life, and not only on a construction site. He recalled an incident that took place in March at his own boarding house, shortly after O.H. Dibble had transferred his family into it.

> A few days after the family moved into our large house, an amusing incident occurred. We had a keg containing 8 or 10 pounds of powder that had been badly wet and dryed [*sic*] into a hard lump. Of course, was of no use, but had not entirely lost its strength.

> Mrs. Dibble had a large fat Dutch girl, that had hurt her ancle [*sic*] and was very lame. They two were sitting before a large wood fire, in the sitting room. The girl wanted something to rest her foot on. She went into the hall, and brought out the keg of damaged

powder, placed it before her, on the hearth, with the open end towards the fire and put her feet on it.

Not long before a spark snapped into the powder, the girl driven back to the wall, Mrs. Dibble thrown from the chair across the room, and the front windows burst out. Strange as it may seem the women were not materially injured but terribly frightened. The big Dutch girl screamed and yelled. Mrs. Dibble thought she was killed. Eventually the event became laughable, and memorable.

In mid-March a second Evans entrepreneur arrived to take charge of a job a few miles upriver of Red Hill, at Peters Mountain. It was 41-year old Aaron Salisbury, the man who a few years previously had convinced the Bennetts to cancel their journey to Ohio and establish themselves in western New York.[14] He arrived with his wife, who was also a Roat sister (23-year-old Ann). "On the first of April," wrote Joseph, "Mr. Salisbury commenced, making preparations on his work by putting up shantees [*sic*], stables, etc. In less than one week, horses, carts and tools were brought and the work commenced."

Possibly Dibble and Salisbury were in partnership, for even though Bennett remained in Dibble's employ, once Salisbury had his operation set up, Bennett left Dibble's job site to serve as clerk and foreman for Salisbury. There was an immediate fatal accident on Salisbury's work site.

> The second day after I left Red Hill, a man, *a very fine man*, was preparing a sand blast, and from some unknown cause, the blast went off, throwing him about four rods into an embankment. Not a bone broken, probably killed by the concussion.
>
> I never allowed anyone to do heavy blasting where I was, on any work, *except myself.*

---

[14] It is likely that Salisbury was involved in construction of the guard lock at Peters Mountain, where canal packets would move between river and canal.

# Constructing the Future

One hot Sunday morning in late July 1827 he was invited by Ann Salisbury, who was almost exactly his age, to go up the mountain near their house to pick huckleberries. "I was stooping over picking berries from a low bush," he said,

> and had an indistinct view of what I supposed was the dropping of cattle, and thoughtlessly careful not to step into it, I saw it stir, and jumped, and as I jumped, the thing rattled and jumped for *me*. I just barely escaped the fangs of a *monster* rattlesnake. He was active and ready for fight, and awfully savage.

As if this five-foot-long rattler was not enough, one week later, in the same huckleberry patch, Bennett and Ann Salisbury ran into a large copperhead. He writes no more of huckleberrying.

Except for the occasional visit of a Catholic priest who said Mass for the Irish upon the canal works, Bennett relates, little else of note happened that summer. "I would sometimes go to Harrisburgh," he wrote, "to see Uncle Seymour and take Mary with me and attend Church. Generally I had enough to do on Sundays to keep up my books. We all worked very hard."

But being 24 years old, he couldn't resist an occasional prank.

> One evening I had been up the river about a quarter of a mile and coming home about 10 o'clock, took it into my head to have a little fun, all to myself. It was *very dark*, dark as Egypt. Sultry, still and warm, not a breath of air stirring. When I came within ten rods of the house where I live, I stopped. Just opposite where I stood, on the other side of road, was a long Irish shantee [*sic*] with no windows in front, made of rough boards, containing 40 or more men, and a few women. I took up a large stone and threw it against the shantee. It made the old thing jingle. The buzzing inside reminded me of a beehive when disturbed. I waited until the noise inside ceased, then threw an-

other large stone, which caused a great disturbance, and commotion.

I waited some minutes until all was quiet again. Then another crash from a stone. I began to think I was the cause of a great amount of sin. Such oaths, such swearing, and, such threats of vengeance, I hardly ever heard. Some came out of doors without dressing, others afraid to come out in the dark for fear of stones (which was wise).

Bennett crept away to his office and went to sleep. "The next morning," he said, "a lot of Irishmen came early, and entered a terrible complaint, that a lot of men had stoned their shanty, and threatened to tear it down over their heads."

But if had not been so dark, they would have gone out and murdered every devil of em. I told them to keep quiet and let me know when they found the rascals. I would have them attended to.

In discussing the basically binational diversity by which he was surrounded, he noted that "the Irish and Germans never could agree very well."

Our teamsters were all Germans. In spite of all we could do there would be some fights. As a rule one Dutchman would whip three Irishmen. The Irish fights are mob fights. But we had two different mills. Each time between two Irishmen, to be fought according to the code, which is very amusing. The combatant strips all but pants. All the Irishmen along the lines come together, go into the field, form a ring, the combatants step into the ring, fold their arms and look at each other. After a little, they loose their arms, and begin to flourish. After a while, one strikes out, no harm, then the other strikes out, no harm. After flourishing again for a time one strikes out, hits the other and his nose bleeds. That ends the mill. The most laughable farce I ever witnessed.

# Constructing the Future

About the middle of October 1827, some "unpleasantness" arose between Joseph and Mr. Dibble, and Bennett either left him or was fired, "very much to the regret of Mr. Salisbury," noted Joseph. Since Bennett had been courting Dibble's sister-in-law, the separation was probably to Bennett's considerable regret as well. Finding work, at least, would not be a problem. A Mr. Green had just arrived, was setting up to build a stone dam across the Susquehanna, and found that Bennett—said to be "the best manager on the lines"—was available.[15] Green told Dibble (within earshot of Joseph) that he intended to hire him, and Dibble began to reconsider his loss.

He invited Joseph to ride with him in his gig, an invitation that Bennett accepted reluctantly, and had a long talk with him. Bennett, evidently uninterested in returning, remained bent on talking to Green, but Dibble, apparently considering the crisis to be over, began to outline the last section of heavy work that remained in their contract, and appeared to assume that Bennett would be overseeing it. Dibble would ensure that he had the horses, tools, and whatever else he needed when he arrived at the work site. The rift was healed, and Bennett took over the job. "I should undoubtedly have engaged with Mr. Green," he said,

> had not things turned as they did. It is passingly strange and I can hardly account for it, why Dibble should be so uncommonly good when he had just treated me as he had.
>
> Whether he was conscience smitten or thot [sic] I would surely get a good position with Mr. Green, I cannot tell. At any rate he was very good. I am sure I was, or had been, very faithful in his business.

---

[15] This dam was designed to create sufficient and dependable depth of river at the Peters Mountain guard lock for canal boats to move between river and canal. Westbound packets exiting the canal and eastbound packets entering it would be pulled across the river behind the dam by mules walking a towpath bridge.

# Joseph Bennett

Bennett seems not to have considered the likely role of the Roat women in Dibble's course of action. One can picture them berating Dibble for his destruction of Mary's marriage prospects. There was no way that Bennett could be allowed to drift out of the Dibble-Roat orbit. O.H. Dibble, who genuinely liked young Bennett and respected his abilities, surely got the point.

Perhaps because of this event, affairs between Joseph and Mary came to a head shortly thereafter. "The most important step in life is now about to be taken," wrote Bennett.

> Mary and I have for months been very much attached to each other but have never made any positive engagement for the present or future, not knowing when circumstances would favor a union, if ever. And now as I am engaged in business, that looks favorable, and that Mr. Dibble's family will soon leave for York State, and that I have no where to live but with the Irish, I now thought Providence had prepared the way for a union, if ever. I explained the situation to Mary and asked her hand, which she readily gave.

Bennett had proposed on Thursday November 1. On the following Sunday they were married.

> Uncle Seymour Bennett and wife, from Harrisburgh, Mr. and Mrs. Salisbury, with a few friends from the near vicinity, met in Mrs. Dibble's parlors at half past one o'clock to witness our marriage at two o'clock P.M., the appointed time. A Presbyterian minister to officiate. For some unaccountable reason, the minister did not come. We waited and waited, finally sent for a judge of the Court. He came and we were married at 4 o'clock P.M. and I believe our Heavenly Father blessed the union.

Mary, he noted, had turned 19 the day before their wedding. He was 24. After a large meal the guests departed, except for Uncle Seymour and wife, who stayed through the next day. Following their departure, Bennett

# Constructing the Future

embarked upon what he wryly described as his and Mary's "wedding tour."

> The second day, Tuesday morning, after the wedding, I went early (4 miles) to my work. There was a large scow lying at the shore of the river, by our work, with a house on it, 26 by 24 feet, fitted up for a store to navagate [sic] up and down the river selling goods. I bought the house and scow but not the goods. In three days time I had the house brought from the scow, put upon a foundation, a partition through the center for bed rooms, and a snug comfortable house we had, ready for house keeping.

> Mary went immediately to work preparing to move . . . *This our wedding tour.*

While Bennett and his new wife were fitting out their first home, Jane Dibble headed back to the Town of Evans, her matchmaking work well done. Coincidentally—as Bennett soon found out in a letter from his father—his sister Rhoda, in Evans, was married at the same hour of the same day as he and Mary. Rhoda's new husband, John Grannis, was as unknown to Joseph as Mary Roat was to the Evans Bennetts.

Many men, once they marry, tend to become conservative and shy away from excessive risk. Not so young Bennett, at least not immediately. "One very cold day in the month of January, 1828," he recalled,

> an Irishman backed a horse and cart off the embankment (we were making) into the river, the water very high and running rapid. As the cart backed from under the lee of the embankment, the current wheeled the whole thing around and headed the horse off shore, he swimming with all his might. The cart fastened to a large boulder, some 20 rods down stream and ten rods from shore. There they were, the poor horse, struggling with all his might, must soon die there unless relieved. The Irishmen gathered upon the shore. One foreman I had, that boasted of his strength but he was powerless. I could not stand

it to see the horse struggle and die there without an effort to save him. There was a little bit of a canoe on the shore near by, I had that brought up far enough to take the advantage of the current. I pushed the canoe over the ice until it went into the slush ice at the edge of the water, then stepped into the canoe, and pushing it through the slush ice, it upset. I then worked through the ice, the men all hallowing, come back youl [sic] *drown, youl die, come back.* I then swam down to the horse, could do nothing with him, the harness new, wet, and very cold, and I had no knife, and the horse strugling [sic], with all his might. I swam ashore, hallowed to them to get me a sharp knife. I took the knife, ran up the shore to where I first started, swam off to the horse, cut the harness and let him loose. We both swam ashore way below.

The excited bystanders caught hold of the horse, and several men rubbed him down at once and got a blanket on him. As for the rescuer, "I was not in a very pleasant condition," he said of his dangerous winter swim in the Susquehanna. "When I reached the house every rag on me was froze stiff. Pretty much spoiled my watch, but saved a valuable horse."

They worked throughout the winter, "fifty men and 15 or 16 horses." In mid-April, with completion of the work only a few months off, Mary left with O.H. Dibble for her new home in the Town of Evans, moving into her brother-in-law's house there. Despite being newly pregnant, the young New Jersey girl succeeded in weathering the six-day stagecoach trip to western New York, where she was unknown and would have to begin the process of integration into a new family and community. Joseph remained in the Susquehanna Valley, pushing the work, intent on finishing it as quickly as possible. He now had at his disposal "a large number of men and forty or more horses."

"Our teamsters and mechanics, waggon makers and blacksmiths," he noted, "were all Germans."

# Constructing the Future

Among our teamsters we had two men, Tom and Bob Vernon, brothers, large, strong, fine young men, were considered the best men we had. Somehow a feud or quarrel arose between them and the Irish. There never is a friendly feeling existing between the Irish and the Germans. The result was a hard fight between the two boys and eight or ten Irishmen. The boys whipped the lot. This was in the evening. The boys left the next morning, or they would have been murdered, and went across the river (1/2 mile wide) and stayed there for two weeks, and would come over dark nights and pound every Irishman they could find and return. This was continued occasionally for two weeks. The whole force of our Irishmen were actually afraid to be out dark nights, unless in large squads.

Work was winding down for all the Evans men. Aaron Salisbury wrapped up his project and went home in the fall. Bennett, with Dibble's crew, would be in Pennsylvania another six months, doubtless a trial to him, since in late October he received word that Mary had given birth to a son, who, in honor of Uncle Seymour Bennett of Harrisburg, was named Seymour.[16] In early November the Dibbles arrived back on the Susquehanna, O.H. moving immediately downriver to Columbia to oversee further work there. The Dibbles would stay until the third week of January 1829 before returning home, leaving Isaiah Gray in charge of the work at Columbia.

The work may have been nearing completion, but prior to Dibble's departure, the Evans men's ability to handle their workers received a test. The trouble appeared to come from the Irish. "In November about the 20th," recalled Bennett,

> there was a strike along the lines. Our work being the largest and more central, men gathered from each way onto our works. Work was entirely stopped for 7

---

[16] Seymour was born October 23, 1828, in the Town of Evans.

or 8 days, higher wages demanded. We refused. We had the sheriff with a company of cavalry and the Catholic Bishop, Curren, from Harrisburgh. A number of the men were arrested and sent to jail. Soon the men came back to work, all we would take at the old price. We procured the release of prisoners.

Bennett's troubles were not over. In mid-February, after Dibble left for home, he received a note from Isaiah Gray at Columbia, 40 miles from Red Hill. Gray said he was "in some little trouble with the men," and asked Bennett to come down immediately to help him sort it out. Bennett, who evidently did not want to ride the 40 miles from his present work at Peters Mountain on horseback, noted that the ground was still covered with wet snow, and thought of a better transportation plan. "The next morning, . . ." he recalled,

> I sent two men after two poles for a jumper, (the sleighing good). I put our waggon maker at the work, making the jumper and stood by superintending. In 2-1/2 hours my carriage was completed, a small dry goods box for a seat.

> With the largest and most beautiful dapple gray horse in all that country hitched to the jumper, I left for Columbia, found things a little mixed with the men but fixed things up nicely.

He had arrived in Columbia at a fortuitous moment, since the canal commissioners and engineers were about to throw a Washington's Birthday party there, and hearing that Bennett was in town, they saw that he received an invitation. "A *select* party," he proudly relates.

The next morning he left on the return trip to Peters Mountain and a much anticipated family reunion there. This reunion would be different, however, since not only would Mary be there, but their new son as well. Eager to see his family, he doubled his horsepower by hitching a second gray in tandem with the first, and headed out of Columbia atop his jumper. "We created as great a sensation," he recalled, "as Barnum's Great Show. My jumper

# Constructing the Future

was a great curiosity in Harrisburg." Stopping in Harrisburg for dinner, he pushed on to Peters Mountain, and beat the arrival of Dibble, the Salisburys, and his wife and new son by an hour. "My wife and baby came," he wrote. "There was great rejoicing."

"Wife and little Seymour were both well," he reported. "All came by stage, most of the way in a chartered coach, fitted up for comfort. Mr. Salisbury going to Washington to assist Mr. Dibble on a Georgetown canal job."

By May, Bennett's work was at last finished. "Took horses, carriages, carts, tools, everything down to Columbia," he recalled.

> Wife and I stayed there 10 or 12 days. Uncle Seymour and family were there. I was quite sick for a few days with bilious fever. Uncle Seymour had painted a number of paintings for us, viz. a portrait for [sic] himself and wife, and my wife, and a landscape.

The Bennetts, following their stay with a Dr. Alden in Columbia, planned to take a leisurely route home: the stage to Philadelphia, followed by a trip to New Jersey, then to New York and finally home via the Hudson River and the Erie Canal. Dr. Alden offered to take them in his carriage the eight miles to Lancaster, where they could catch the stage to Philadelphia. Jane Dibble, as well as Uncle Seymour and wife, would accompany them to the stage stop in Lancaster. The trip nearly ended before it began.

The road to Lancaster lay over a "hilly, paved turnpike," recounted Bennett.

> I had been over the road before and knew exactly how the road was situated. The morning of our departure we left in a very nice carriage, open in front, covered behind. Dr. and myself sitting in front seat, horses pretty wild; Dr. driving, Uncle Seymour and wife in a gig accompanying. We were getting along very nicely for two or three miles. All at once, while going down a

sharp hill, both holdbacks gave way.[17]   The horses frightened and ran with a vengeance, it seemed every minute that the carriage would surely go in pieces over the paved road. I saw the horses were becoming unmanageable, and the Dr. not a good driver. I took the lines from his hands.

The reaction of the two women and seven-month-old baby in the back seat is not recorded. "There was now," related Bennett,

a sharp rise in the road for 20 or 25 rods to the top of a hill. At the top, smooth level rock for over 100 feet, then a steep down grade for at least one hundred rods to a toll gate. At the top of the hill, a sharp ridge had been quarried off to grade the road and to furnish paving stone, leaving a perpendicular wall of solid rock at either side of the flat surface of 20 feet. Now having the lines, thought that perhaps I might stop the horses before reaching the top, knowing that we should all be destroyed going down the hill. But could not, destruction seemed inevitable.

As he had done when describing how he'd almost blown himself up by dropping a candle into a keg of black powder, he commented again, "Thoughts run quick."

To go on—all lost. To turn short against the wall might save some of us. Like a flash it was done, and so rapidly that the carriage slewed round and upset. The horses in trying to turn, as they butted the wall, were thrown over on to their backs as the carriage upset. Mrs. Dibble, my wife, and baby were thrown out from the carriage. The off horse in trying to turn was thrown over on the near side, with his feet up. Women and horses all together. I pulled the women and baby from under the horses, while the Dr. held

---

[17] Holdbacks are straps attached between the horses' harness and the carriage shaft to keep the vehicle from running into the horses when going downhill or backing.

the horses heads. Seems to me a most wonderful escape. Mrs. Dibble, baby, Dr., and myself not hurt a particle. Mary's head bruised some . . . She was soon able to be arround [sic], and walked down to the toll gate.

Uncle Seymour and wife drove up in a froth, related Joseph, "awfully frightened, supposing we were badly injured if not killed."

"We now made an examination of the wreck," he continued,

found horses and harness uninjured, carriage injured to the extent of perhaps $5.00. After putting every thing in order, harness made secure, I mounted the carriage and drove down to the toll gate where all *reluctantly* took the carriage and went to Lancaster.

Staying overnight in Lancaster, the still-shaken young couple and resilient baby Seymour took the stage to Philadelphia next day, purchasing there a "good watch and two sett [sic] of silver spoons" (the watch likely to replace the one ruined in the Susquehanna the previous winter). The following day they boarded a steamer for a trip up the Delaware to Bordentown, New Jersey, just south of Trenton, where they arranged for a carriage to take them inland to Englishtown and a visit to Mary's parents. "While at Bordentown waiting for our carriage," noted Bennett, "the beautiful daughter of the hotel keeper seemed to take quite a fancy to our baby Seymour."

They left after the noonday meal, arriving at Englishtown about 4 in the afternoon, and entered into a pleasant ten-day stay with "Mother and Father Roat."

"In a day or two," recalled Joseph, "saw the startling announcement 'Murder in High Life.' The daughter of the wealthy Mr. _____ of Bordentown, shot and killed by a rejected suitor. I cannot now recall the name of the lady, it is her that played with Seymour a few days since."

At the end of their stay, Father and Mother Roat took them by carriage to the coast, where they boarded a

# Joseph Bennett

steamer for New York, and the following day a steamer up the Hudson to Albany. They then took an evening stage to Schenectady, where at midnight they boarded a canal packet for the final leg of their trip to Buffalo.

Bennett appeared to enjoy canal travel thoroughly. He had never, he said, found "a more delightful way of traveling" than on the canal packet. "It is amusing," he said, "to see the amount of style on one of these little boats." It must indeed have been a pleasant way to travel. A contemporary novelist, Nathaniel Parker Willis, in describing Erie Canal travel, wrote that

> no traveller sees a greater variety of fine objects within the same distance than the follower of the Canal from Schenectady to Buffalo; and certainly none sees them with more ease and comfort to himself. The packet-boats are long drawing-rooms, where he dines, sleeps, reads, lolls, or looks out of the window; and if in want of exercise, he may at any time get a quick walk on the tow-path, and all this without perceptible motion, jar, or smell of steam.[18]

The little family arrived in Buffalo harbor on June 27, 1829—almost nine years to the day since Joseph had first sighted Buffalo—and next day took the stage to the Town of Evans, where he was reunited with his parents and his nine brothers and sisters, whom he had not seen in three years. Once the stories had been swapped and the neighbors had been greeted and the familiar fields and beaches had been walked, Joseph found time to think seriously about the next step.

"After resting two or three days," he recalled, "began to think what to do next. Must hunt up some business and locate somewhere." Canal construction was completed now in western New York and was by then being carried out only in places far from home. In any case, Bennett had lost interest in being away from home. He

---

[18] Nathaniel Parker Willis, *American Scenery, or, Land, Lake, and River: Illustrations of Transatlantic Nature,* (London: George Virtue, 1839) 119.

was a family man now, and wanted to raise his new family near his old family, a decision in which Mary seems to have concurred. She would, after all, be near her sisters as well. Lake commerce would not be his path, although he was immensely pleased to be back on Lake Erie's shore. Farming made sense. He could certainly feed a family on farming, and might even make money at it.

The 25-year-old Bennett, who had evidently made enough in Pennsylvania to get a decent start, already knew the piece of land that he wanted.

He stopped over to talk to James Aldrich about the 189-acre farm that he had for sale along the lower reaches of Big Sister Creek.

BATTLE OF PLATTSBURGH, SEPTEMBER 11, 1814 – Joseph Bennett heard the sounds of this Lake Champlain naval battle from the protection of a blockhouse 20 miles away in Jay, Essex County, New York. Through superior tactics, aided by good fortune, a hastily formed American fleet defeated a Royal Navy squadron in what proved to be a pivotal engagement for the outcome of the war. This painting was made in 1884 by Julian O. Davidson.

*Source: Chipman P. Turner,* The Pioneer Period of Western New York

TYPICAL HOME OF SETTLER, HOLLAND PURCHASE, WESTERN NEW YORK STATE – These tiny homes were primitive in the extreme. Early settlers on the Purchase endured unimaginable hardships. Trees were at once their friend and foe. Note field of stumps. This picture represents a homestead in its third year of development. Such homes were still being hewn out of the Niagara Frontier wilderness when the Bennetts arrived in 1820, although their first home, a log structure with 15 cleared acres, was more advanced than this.

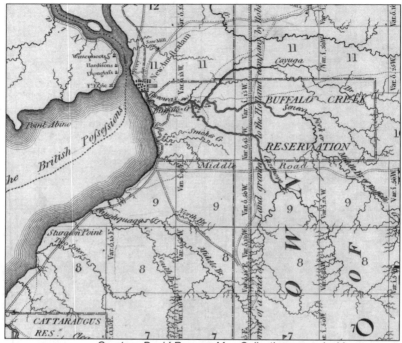

A PORTION OF WESTERN NEW YORK IN 1800 – A rudimentary road system is already in place. Middle Road is present-day Big Tree Road, leading ultimately to Big Tree near Geneseo. Buffalo was at the time known as New Amsterdam. The Buffalo Creek reservation, about seven miles wide, extended almost 20 miles eastward from the lake, to the present-day Wyoming County line. Joseph Bennett arrived in Buffalo 20 years after this map was drawn.

*Source: Truman C. White, ed.,* Our County and its People: A Descriptive Work on Erie County New York.

BUFFALO HARBOR IN 1816 – View at the mouth of Buffalo Creek. The village of Buffalo was by this time recovered from the devastation of December 1813, and on the road to great prosperity. This view is similar to what Joseph Bennett must have seen upon his family's arrival in Buffalo four years later, although by this time efforts had commenced to improve the creek entrance for the entry of deep-draft vessels.

*Courtesy Chittenango Landing Canal Boat Museum*

THE ERIE CANAL AT LOCKPORT, LATE 1820s – At Lockport, westbound canal traffic had to be lifted over the 65-foot-high Niagara Escarpment, and eastbound traffic eased down it. A series of five double locks, visible at right center, was constructed to accomplish this. Joseph Bennett participated in this construction effort. Details of this modern painting by Dr. Robert E. Hager are supported by period depictions.

CROSSING THE STATE IN STYLE – This scene, painted by Dr. Robert E. Hager and set near Little Falls in central New York, captures the beauty of canal travel in the late 1820s and 1830s. The canal packets, pulled by mules, afforded many comforts. Passengers needing to stretch their legs could get off and walk beside the boat if they wished. Joseph Bennett and his wife made use of this elegant, if slow, mode of travel on more than one occasion.

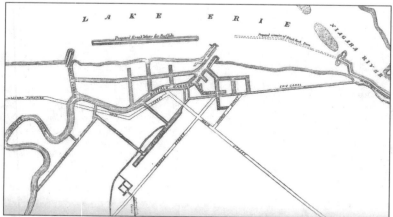

Source: Truman C. White, ed., Our County and its People: A Descriptive Work on Erie County New York.

BUFFALO WATERFRONT IN 1836 – Map shows proposed improve-ments, as well as plan of South Channel, running (at upper left) between creek and lake. Joseph Bennett supervised construction of this channel the previous year. It is unclear if the project was completed at this time. North is to right.

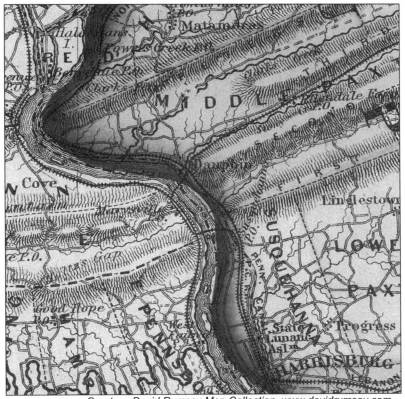

*Courtesy David Rumsey Map Collection, www.davidrumsey.com*

DAUPHIN COUNTY ON THE SUSQUEHANNA, NORTH OF
HARRISBURG, PENNSYLVANIA – Joseph Bennett spent 1826-29 as a
construction foreman in Middle Paxton and Reed Townships on the Susquehanna's east bank. He and his men labored in the Eastern Division of
Pennsylvania's budding canal system, built at great expense and rendered
obsolete almost at once by the railroads. Bennett's sphere of responsibility
was principally along the river in Middle Paxton township. At Clark's Ferry
(upper left), north of Peters Mountain, the canal joined the river, where
mules on a towpath bridge would pull packet boats across the Susquehanna to or from the Juniata River, west of the islands at the top of the
map. The map was made in 1872.

*Source: Frederick W. Beers,* Illustrated Historical Atlas of Erie County

A PORTION OF THE TOWN OF EVANS, NEW YORK, IN 1880 – The map shows the boundaries of Joseph Bennett's original 189 acres along the lake, although by the time this map was drawn he had transferred two parcels to his son Judson and one to Hiram Backus. The lower reaches of Big Sister Creek are inaccurately drawn. West of the Lake Shore Road, the creek bent sharply to the north before entering the lake.

*Courtesy Town of Evans Historical Society*

FIRST BAPTIST CHURCH OF EVANS, EVANS CENTER, NY – Deacon Joseph Bennett was a moving force in the founding of this church in 1830, and remained active in its ministry for his entire life. Stained-glass windows bearing the names of Joseph and Mary Bennett and other members of the Bennett family remain as graceful reminders of the family's love for this later structure, dedicated in April 1856. This photo dates from the 1920s.

# 5

# *ERIE COUNTY CITIZEN*

It was probably with some trepidation that Joseph went to see former town supervisor Aldrich about the property, since it was the same cherished "beautiful flat" that he had discovered nine years earlier on his first exploration of the area. The opportunity to own this land was a dream come true. He found his neighbor willing to sell, but disappointingly uncompromising on price. Given Bennett's great interest in the property, and his readily available resources, it is surprising that he would not meet Aldrich's price. For his entire stock, horses, carriages, tools, buildings, land, and crops, Aldrich wanted $3,750; Bennett offered him $3,500, and there the matter stood. Next day, Bennett, apparently philosophical about the loss, bought a horse and buggy so that he and Mary could start looking elsewhere. But, "in the morning," he relates,

> just as we were about starting, Mr. Aldrich came to see me, said he had concluded to accept my offer. I then agreed to take the farm, 189 acres of land, 6 cows, 6 horses, 1 yoke oxen, 40 sheep, some young stock, some hogs, waggon and harness, ploughs, drags, all the tools of every kind. On the 6th day of July, 1829, deed signed, money paid over.[19] Wife and

---

[19] The Erie County deed book records Bennett's purchase of 189 acres from James and Hannah Aldrich as occurring on August 6,

I were now installed agriculturists, farmers, and must go immediately into housekeeping. Before we left Harrisburgh, I bot [sic] a large Bible which is all we have to commence on. As soon as the farm was paid for we went to Buffalo for furnature [sic], etc., viz. 1/2 blb. whiskey, bedding, crockery, chairs, tables, everything necessary, and moved into our house. Hired a man and girl *and at it we went* at farming.

Mary, he notes, "without any experience, is a *model* housekeeper."

Aldrich, who apparently was depending on the money from the sale of the property to purchase a new home, for the moment had nowhere to go. Bennett offered to let the Aldriches stay with them until winter if they wished. It is unclear whether Aldrich took him up on the offer.

Bennett, his life having changed very quickly from traveling canal contractor to established farmer and citizen, looked around himself and took stock. "Here we are now in a new country," he noted,

> roads about as bad as roads can be. Our house small and unfinished, 1-1/2 story high, 26 x 26. Small barn, 140 acres wild, timbered land, only fifty acres cleared land. What an amount of *work* to be done to put the farm in a desirable, and available, condition.

"We think," he concluded, "we have the ability, and energy, to accomplish it."

One of his first actions was to subscribe $100 toward repair of the road that crossed his land.[20] "All the in-

---

not July 6, and for a price of $3,000, not $3,500. It further records a purchase by Bennett a month earlier, on July 7, of 50 acres just northeast of the 189-acre tract. This property was purchased directly from the Holland Land Company for $225. Available maps do not show Bennett's ownership of the smaller parcel, and Bennett does not mention either buying or selling it.

[20] This would be the present Lake Shore Road, which did not follow its modern path around today's Bennett Beach park, but crossed Bennett's land closer to the lake. The road to Evans Center, today's Bennett Road, therefore joined the Lake Shore Road in

habitants," he continued, "paid or worked according to their ability [to repair the road]. The main travel has been, and is, on the beach of the lake. Will soon have a good road on the land." He recalls the wonderful spot that he had discovered on arrival in November 1820, and concludes proudly, "We now own it."

Seeming to have a ready supply of money, he tackled improvements with a vengeance. The following summer, 1830, he built a 30-foot long addition to the south side of the house for a kitchen and woodhouse, and added a parlor on the north side. "We tore down the stack of chimneys," he recorded,

> and put up new. The house being unfinished, had it lathed and plastered, and fixed up generally. Also had a very nice front, and yard, fence quite expensively built. We also had a large barn and cattle stable put up. Our buildings now being pretty good, turned our attention to clearing land and farming.

He contracted, at $15 an acre, to have 10 acres of woods on one lot cleared and five on another, but complained about his lack of ability to dispose of cut timber, likely because the roads were too poor to transport it easily. One could therefore clear only as much timber as one could use. This was a hard country to commence in, he noted, but—striking his habitual note of optimism—it would eventually be a "fine old country."

The Erie Canal having been in operation for nearly five years, new settlers were streaming into Buffalo. Many were pushing out along the lake shore to Evans and beyond. Several families arrived that year from St.

---

the middle of today's park rather than at its eastern edge, as it does today. Bennett's property, of course, was not restricted to the modern park, but stretched (on both sides of the Lake Shore Road) from approximately the mouth of Big Sister Creek (the creek then emptying into the lake further north than it does today) southwestward to Lake Bay, a little beyond today's Bay Point Road. Doubtless Bennett was concerned with road improvement through this entire area.

# Joseph Bennett

Lawrence County—three families of Barretts, three of Rowleys, three of Atwoods, and several others. "Nearly all of them were Baptists," noted Joseph, who was conceiving an interest at this time in being baptized into the Baptist Church. The problem was that there was no church in the Town of Evans. It would have to be founded.

Joseph encountered others interested in organizing a church. "On the 23rd of July," he wrote, "a meeting of those desiring an organization of a Baptist Church was held at the Evans Center school house.[21] The meeting unanimous in favor of a church organization." In September the group met again, and "adopted articles of Faith and Covenant with a membership of eleven." The following January (1831) a council from the Baptist Churches in the regional association convened "to consider the propriety of recognizing the church in the fellowship of the Baptist denomination" at Evans Center.

"It being a terrible tedious, cold day, only the delegates from the Fredonia and Dunkirk churches were present," recalled Bennett. "The council however did organize. Eld[er] Elisha Tucker from Fredonia. The articles of Faith were approved by the council."

Following the approval of the articles of Faith and Practice and Covenant by the council, Phebe, the young wife of Bennett's 23-year-old brother Alonzo, was baptized in the frigid waters of Big Sister Creek. "The day being intensely cold," recalled her brother-in-law, "a place for baptism was made through very thick ice . . . After baptism the hand of fellowship was given to the new church." In August 1832 Bennett himself and his wife Mary were baptized, along with ten others. His mother, his sisters Rhoda and Sarah, and his brothers Sam and Thomas all became members of the church, which, under the guiding hand of Elder Jonathan Hascall, prospered and grew from the beginning. In May

---

[21] The Evans Center schoolhouse mentioned is not the one at Evans Center today. The latter was built in 1857.

# Erie County Citizen

1834 the 30-year-old Bennett was appointed Deacon, and was forever after referred to as Deacon Bennett by his neighbors. ("Rather poor material," he quipped, in reference to this appointment.) He also took over as superintendent of the Sabbath school, where he would supervise the religious education of children for the next 40 years.

Like the church, the Bennett family itself was growing and prospering. On October 4, 1830, Mary had given birth to a girl whom she named Jane, and on January 9, 1833, a second girl had been born, this one to be called Henrietta. The Bennetts now had three children, the eldest of whom was four.

This was the time of cholera in Buffalo. In the summer of 1832—the very year of Buffalo's incorporation as a city—death carts were being pushed through the streets. Cholera would stalk these same streets again in 1834, filling hospitals and homes with scenes of illness and death. The mayor of Buffalo himself (Major A. Andrews) would succumb. The disease, thought to have been brought to Buffalo from Canada by the tide of immigrants sweeping into the city—and surely abetted by the sanitary conditions of the time—killed over one hundred people in the summer of 1832 and made many more seriously ill. Bennett does not mention this epidemic, but it is likely that travel to Buffalo from outlying towns was curtailed during this period.

"During summer 1834," noted Bennett laconically, "engaged in farming pursuits exclusively."

In the late fall of 1833, Bennett's parents had followed through on their original dream of moving to the west. They pulled up stakes in Evans and, presumably with most of their ten children, headed to southern Michigan, "about as far west as land is offered for sale by government," explained Joseph. His parents were by this time in their fifties. It is unclear what prompted this move, but Samuel Sr. had stayed in Evans longer than he had stayed anywhere, and it must have seemed time to move on. There is some evidence that he was following the lead of neighbors who had moved west. At any rate, his daughter-in-law and eldest son lost little time in heading west to visit Samuel and Sally in their new home, near Niles, Michigan.[22]

In September 1834, leaving their two youngest behind, he and Mary, along with Bennett's sister Rhoda and her husband John Grannis, and accompanied by veteran traveler 5-year-old Seymour, departed for Michigan. Mary was pregnant with their fourth child.[23] As an indication either of a remarkable improvement in the new nation's roads, or of the little group's astonishing tolerance of discomfort, they traveled all the way in a two-horse carriage, taking ten days to travel out and ten days back. They found "a beautiful country nearly all the way through Ohio and Michigan," reported Bennett, "government land $1.25 per acre." They were gone a month.

During these years, Bennett's connection with O.H. Dibble proved a continuing source of benefit. The previous summer, Dibble, by now a retired town supervisor, and currently serving as Evans postmaster, was appointed postmaster at Buffalo and had to vacate his Evans position. He saw to it, however, that the Evans appointment went to young Bennett. Dibble, who had enjoyed continued success at sniffing out construction jobs, showed also that he hadn't forgotten Bennett's value as a construction superintendent. In the spring of 1835 the older man was awarded a contract to cut a channel from Buffalo Creek, just above the creek's mouth, due west to the lake—the so-called South Channel—and he asked young Bennett to superintend the work for him. Additionally, Dibble had been contracted to work on a new Baptist church being constructed on Washington Street, as well as on two brick houses ad-

---

[22] In 1837 Samuel would buy 24 acres in present-day Mishawaka, Indiana, just over the Michigan state line.
[23] Judson O. Bennett would be born January 7, 1835.

joining the church, projects for which he sought Bennett's services in gathering building materials.[24]

On top of his farming and now post office responsibilities, and with a growing family, Joseph was kept busy at Dibble's job sites in Buffalo until spring 1836.

The Bennetts' fifth and last child, Josephine, was born on February 18, 1837, a year that marked the beginning of a period of great trial for the family. Sometime in 1837, possibly after the birth of her daughter, Mary had noticed a lump in her breast. She and Joseph consulted physicians, probably locally and in Buffalo, but to no avail. The larger the tumor grew, the more certain they became that it was cancerous. "All medical aid," said Joseph, "has been of no avail and slowly getting worse."

> We were terribly alarmed, and had almost given up hope of her ever being any better, when we saw in the Baptist Register an advertisement of a cancer doctor in the Town of Locke, Cayuga Co.

He immediately wrote to the "Dr. Lynch" of the ad, and by mid-May had received a response. There was no hesitation in taking Mary to see this unknown practitioner, since, as Bennett declared, "In our extremity we catch at any thing."

"On the 18th of May, 1838," he recounted, "we left home, went to Buffalo in a carriage, took a canal boat in Buffalo for Montezuma, then up Cayuga Lake to Aurora, then to Locke."

He was in familiar territory—Locke lies about halfway between his beloved Cayuga Lake and present-day I-81

---

[24] The Baptist church in question was the architecturally elegant Washington Street Baptist Church, successor to the First Baptist Church of Buffalo. The latter had been erected at Seneca and Washington Streets in 1828, but was shortly thereafter sold. It came to be used first as a post office, and later as the first University of Buffalo medical school. The Washington Street Baptist Church, which Bennett helped construct at Washington and Swan, was razed in 1900.

south of Syracuse—and at the conclusion of their journey he was relieved to find a medical man who betrayed no lack of confidence in his curative powers. "Found the Dr.," he wrote. "I trembled before his answer during the examination," but, as he affirmed, the doctor said he could cure her.

Bennett made arrangements for Mary to remain in Locke for treatment, boarding with Dr. Lynch. A price was agreed upon: $20 to cover the treatment, payable in advance, and $20 following a perfect cure. Mary's board would be extra.

Bennett returned home to his five children, ages 9 years to 15 months, doubtless praying fervently, hoping against hope for his young wife's recovery. Whatever the treatment was—likely surgery, or possibly a proprietary concoction better left undescribed to the patient—it caused her significant suffering, as she reported to Joseph in her three letters per week. Mary remained in Locke for six weeks, finally returning to Buffalo on her own via the canal.

"I met her there," exulted Joseph, "and brot [sic] her home in a carriage. A regular *Jubilee* when we arrived home."

Joseph, of cautious nature, waited until December 1840, fully two and a half years after Mary's return, before sending Dr. Lynch the remainder of his fee. Both he and Mary were satisfied by this time that she was no longer ill, and in fact a full life remained to her.

Erie County saw the beginnings of phenomenal growth in the 1830s, witnessing a population jump during the decade's first five years of from 35,719 to 57,594 (Buffalo's population surged from about 9,000 to 20,000 in the same period.) Buffalo's Canal Street, coming to be known as the "wickedest street in the world," was filled with both strangers and locals seeking pleasure in the many saloons, dance halls, and brothels that lined it. A portion of Main Street in Buffalo was actually being paved, and the future looked rosy for anyone who wanted to be part of this explosive growth. Joseph's year of construction in 1835-36 was a direct result of the building boom in Buffalo at this time. And despite the revolution in transportation brought about by the canal, an even farther-reaching revolution—one that would unfortunately be the canal's death-knell—was arriving. It was advancing on a set of parallel iron rails. In 1836, a set of primitive tracks was laid between Black Rock and Tonawanda (soon to be extended to Niagara Falls), and a steam locomotive and rail cars were brought in. With no extant body of knowledge in railroad construction, the tracks were so poorly laid that they suffered frost heave and quickly became unusable except for careful pulling of the cars by horses. More substantial tracks were soon laid in their place, and Buffalo's first rail link to anywhere was a reality.

By early 1843, the growing city would have its first rail connection to the east, with the opening of the Buffalo and Attica railroad, the final link in a chain of connected roads reaching across the state from Albany.[25] Westward and southward travel would continue to be by boat or stage for nearly another decade.

Despite this progress and promise for the future, these were anxious times on the Niagara Frontier. The great speculation accompanying the exuberant expansion of the nation led to a widespread financial crash in 1837, doubtless bursting a number of carefully blown bubbles in this busy port city. Added to the business malaise, the region, incredibly, found itself at the center of a burgeoning war.

Known as the Patriots' War, it began in November 1837 as a rising in Canada of largely ethnic French Canadians against the British Crown. The movement quickly spread to equally dissatisfied subjects in British Canada, a number of whom sought refuge in Buffalo fol-

---

[25] Within a few years the rail link to Albany would reduce Buffalo-Albany travel time from six days to 25 hours.

# Joseph Bennett

lowing skirmishes that month with loyalists in Toronto. Many Buffalonians (including some political leaders), remembering their city's burning by the British a quarter-century before, were sympathetic to the rebel cause and displayed their sentiments by providing the uprising's leader, William Lyon Mackenzie, with money, supplies, and arms (some likely "lifted" from New York State arsenals). Emboldened by this support, Mackenzie and his followers moved in December to occupy Canada's Navy Island in the west branch of the Niagara, off the northwest tip of Grand Island. Loyalists outraged by American support of this blatant affront to the Crown crossed the river, seized an American ship near the present-day New York Power Authority intakes, set it afire, and cast it adrift. The United States government responded by beefing up garrisons at Buffalo and along the river, and by sending General Winfield Scott to take charge of them personally. When in January 1838 Mackenzie abandoned Navy Island, tempers on both sides of the border began to cool.

Despite a slight easing of tension along the Niagara Frontier, a lesson had been learned, and U.S. defensive preparations continued in earnest. In the fall of 1839, an imposing new army barracks was constructed in Buffalo between Delaware Avenue and Main Street, extending from Allen to North. One infantry and two artillery regiments were brought in, sequentially, to man the new post, and western New York males showed themselves responsive to the call of duty.

In 1839, Joseph Bennett—with his experience in construction, explosives, and managing men—was elected lieutenant of an artillery company, and in 1840, captain. Since national feelings continued to improve, he never saw active service.

It was these years that marked the beginning of Joseph's entry into local and eventually county and state affairs. In 1843 the 39-year old Bennett was appointed executor of the estate of Aaron Atwood, Jr., and guardian of Atwood's minor son Leroy. In the same year he took two other children under his wing: he was appointed executor of the estate of Annis Seeley and guardian of her two minor sons, John and Thaddeus, the latter of whom would one day become his son-in-law. He would be named executor of other estates in the Town of Evans.

Two years later, in 1845, Bennett was elected to his first term as Town of Evans supervisor, the term of office at this time being one year.[26] In the same year he was elected county coroner, a post that required no medical knowledge, and that empowered its occupant to summon inquest juries to assist in determining the cause of death—to determine, at the very least, whether a death had been by natural causes, accident, suicide, or homicide.[27] Other duties were also involved, as in investigating accidents where no loss of life was at issue.

It is unknown if he still served as town postmaster during this period.

It appears that, for some years past, Bennett's younger brother Laban had been afflicted with tuberculosis. A crisis must have arisen in the summer of 1844 because Bennett rushed to southwest Michigan to see his brother. "Found him very low," he noted, "did not think he could live but a few days." After spending the better part of a week with Laban and the rest of his family, Joseph headed home, only to find out that Laban had passed away on the third day following his departure. He had been only 27 years old.

---

[26] Supervisors were elected in the spring at an annual Town Meeting. Bennett would be reelected in 1846, 1847, 1848, 1852, and 1878. In 1852 he would serve as chairman of the Erie County Board of Supervisors.

[27] New York state law still requires no medical degree or advanced education for the office of coroner. A medical examiner, on the other hand, must have a degree in medicine, with specialized training in forensic pathology.

# Joseph Bennett

♧

Anyone living on the shores of Lake Erie even today knows that autumn winds can turn the lake into a powerful agent for damage, whether to shoreline structures or to vessels that have been disabled, or that simply are not suited to the energy level of wind and wave. Modern lake freighters, guided by accurate weather reports, having suitable harbors at hand, and being built to withstand Great Lakes fury, are seldom victimized. One today may hear of an occasional day-sailor accident, but—apart from the case of the 729-foot *Edmund Fitzgerald*, lost on Lake Superior in 1975—one no longer hears of the capsizing or sinking of a Great Lakes commercial vessel. Not so in the 1840s, when the main path to the west was the centerline of Lake Erie, and when hundreds of old or inadequate vessels—some steam-driven, some under sail—plied these waters.

Sometime during the daylight hours of October 18, 1844, an unusually strong southwester started to blow. By midnight it was piling a wall of water into the port of Buffalo, causing the destruction of dock facilities, flooding shoreline property to a depth of several feet, and scattering lumber and debris throughout the harbor. A number of the unwitting, many of them asleep, were caught by the standing wave and drowned. The wind did not soon blow itself out. Between October 18 and October 20, four ships in eastern Lake Erie were either sunk or blown ashore and wrecked. They were the wooden schooner *Pennsylvania*, which on October 18 capsized and went down with all hands off Barcelona; the 80-foot schooner *Pacific*, which, on the same date, was blown ashore and broke apart near Dunkirk; the 69-foot schooner *Dayton*, which on October 20 capsized and sank off Dunkirk; and the 139-foot side-wheel passenger steamer *Robert Fulton*, which on October 20 became disabled 14 miles east of Dunkirk and was driven hard onto Joseph Bennett's beach.

"In the year 1844 in October," recalled Bennett,

the passenger steamer *Robert Fulton* (Capt. Atwood Master) came ashore on our land. Sometime during the night of one of the most severe gales on record. She became disabled (outside) in the terrible sea. The engine became disabled, and the vessel left entirely at the mercy of wind and waves was driven high upon the beach. When the gale was over, she was over three rods from the water. One child (small child) perished in a berth. When the steamer struck the beach, Capt. Atwood ordered the cabin doors on the main deck opened *which had been closed and fastened for over twenty hours.* Immediately a lady with her daughter came out of her cabin holding each other by the hand. Just then a tremendous swell rolled upon the deck. As the water receded, drew the mother and daughter to the gangway. The mother catched her arm around a stanchion, held her daughter with all her power, but the rush of water tore her away and was lost. Daughter 13 years old. Terribly sad.

Sadness would soon drop its mantle closer to home: on October 13, 1845, Mary's mother Margaret (who had by this time moved with her husband Michael from New Jersey to the Town of Evans) died at the age of 70. And on July 22, 1846, Bennett's father Samuel died, at the age of 69, in New Buffalo, Michigan.[28] "He was taken with congestion of the lungs," wrote Joseph, "only sick three days."

"He was a good man," continued Bennett,

---

[28] New Buffalo, Michigan, had been founded in the 1830s by Buffalo lake-freighter captain Wessel D. Whittaker. In 1834 Whittaker had, in a violent Lake Michigan storm, grounded his schooner at present-day Grand Beach, Michigan, near the Michigan-Indiana state line. On passing northward to report the loss to his underwriters at St. Joseph, Whittaker was struck by the beauty of the shoreline north of Grand Beach. He purchased a large tract of land there, sold a half-interest to his employers in Buffalo, and began to develop it as New Buffalo.

respected by every man, woman, and child, that knew him. Untiring in his efforts for the benefits of his numerous children . . . All grew to be men and women and not a blot or stain upon any one of them. Most of them profess the religion of our Blessed Saviour.

Joseph did not journey to Michigan, since, by the time he received word of his father's death, Samuel would no doubt have been buried. The family of twelve was now ten.

In 1840 a law had been passed in Albany authorizing the Board of Supervisors of Erie County to erect a penitentiary and workhouse for prisoners convicted of minor crimes—men for whom there was no room in the jail, and who had not committed offenses serious enough to be sent to state prison. In 1846, the largely stone building was constructed on present-day Lakeview Avenue between Pennsylvania and (today's) Jersey Streets on Buffalo's west side. Supervisor Bennett, with his experience as a contractor, was appointed one of the commissioners of the new penitentiary, doubtless to supply competent county supervision over its builders. In 1847 or 1848 Bennett and another commissioner signed a contract on the county's behalf with a startup company, Pratt and Letchworth, manufacturers of saddlery and carriage hardware at the time, for the use of prison labor in the company's operation. Workshops were built into the prison for the purpose.

"Was necessary to spend considerable time at the penitentiary," recalled Joseph.

In 1849 cholera revisited the growing city of Buffalo with a vengeance, striking an estimated 3,000 people, nearly 900 of whom succumbed. The disease does not seem to have touched the Bennetts. Death, however, did strike the family the following January, with the passing of Sally Bennett, Joseph's 70-year-old mother. Joseph's remembrance of his mother:

A faithful, devoted, Christian, loving mother. She has labored and toiled for her children, often under adverse circumstances. Never was a strong woman, but had ever so much *determination* and energy.

Sally Bennett was laid to rest at her husband's side in New Buffalo, Michigan.

By 1850, the population of Erie County had reached 101,000, and that of the Town of Evans about 2,200. Largely because of improved stump pullers, both agriculture and overland transportation were taking a major step forward. The removal of stumps from a road was, however, easier than the drainage of water, and portions of roads throughout the county remained impassable morasses at certain times of the year. The laying of closely spaced plank atop the mud made these sections passable, and it was around 1850 that a number of roads in western New York were planked.

In May or June 1850, an opportunity arose for the 46-year-old Evans builder and former supervisor to bid on construction of a plank road over a 2- or 3-mile stretch of present-day Route 5 from Smith's Hotel, out the lake road, probably terminating near present-day Cloverbank.[29] He was awarded the job in June, but it did not go well. The planks, to be supplied by the plank road company that had contracted his services, did not arrive for three months, and then were not supplied steadily enough to meet his needs. "On the 2d day of September," he wrote,

> commenced work on the plank road, continued the work under some hindrances for the want of plank and material from the plank road co., which was a great damage, as it was getting late in the season, *bad weather*, short days, and land wet, etc. On the 2d

---

[29] It is unclear where Smith's Hotel was. The description of the location given in the journal ("8 miles west of Buffalo") fits today's Dock at the Bay restaurant on the lake shore at Bay View Road.

day of November finished, and notified the company. They called the P.R. inspectors, who came, examined the work, and pronounced it good.

The project nonetheless ended on a sour note: "I handed in claims for damage for being delayed for want of material," recalled Joseph, "and am partially remunerated, only to the amount of $100.00."

While the need for plank roads for local travel remained real, in the year or so following Bennett's plank road work, Erie County would become connected to the west by a road made not of plank but of iron. (The area was already connected to Albany, and by the following year would be connected by two lines to New York.) By January 1852 a portion of the single-track Buffalo and State Line Railroad would be opened from Dunkirk to the Pennsylvania line, and the following month the section from Dunkirk to Buffalo would open. The railroad, which would become part of the Lake Shore and Michigan Southern prior to being taken over by the New York Central, would, for the first time in the history of the Niagara Frontier, enable travelers to move west out of Buffalo in reasonable comfort, instead of being pulled for days behind a team of horses over rutted roads, or having to chance a lengthy lake voyage by sail or steam.[30]

But in 1850 the road had not yet been built. The route was being surveyed, and landowners along the route were being dealt with. Land taken for right-of-way had to be assessed for compensation, and Joseph Bennett, in the midst of his contract on the plank road, found himself called upon to help. "On the 31st day of August, 1850," he recounted,

> I received notice from the officials of the L.S.R.R. [Lake Shore Railroad] Co. that I am appointed R.R. appraiser to appraise damages along the line of R.R. together with Albert H. Tracy, Ralph Plumb, and oth-

---

[30] In 1845, Great Lakes steamers carried more than 93,000 passengers.

ers. A number of days occupied in appraising damages along the line during Sept. and October.[31]

Former Supervisor Bennett's evident competence in everything he touched was by this time becoming recognized by western New York power brokers, and in September 1850—again, while he was walking the railroad right-of-way with a group of appraisers and trying to get a plank road built in the Town of Hamburg—he was asked if he would consider running as the district's Whig candidate for state assembly.[32]   He said yes, but with misgivings. "On the 21st day of September, 1850," he wrote,

> I attended the Assembly District Convention at Boston, called to nominate a Member of Assembly. The name of C.C. Severance of Springville, and my name, were presented to the convention for nomination. The first vote taken at 2 o'clock P.M. was a tie. The vote was taken as often as every 20 minutes until about sundown, still a tie. I requested my friends *often* during the afternoon, to withdraw my name but they said *no*, Col. Plumb being the leading man for me. Just before sundown withdrew my name, thanked my friends and recommended Mr. Severance. Mr. Severance is a good man, and competent.[33]

---

[31] Albert H. Tracy was a former U.S. congressman and state senator, the same who had shared the 16-year-old Bennett's stagecoach from Union Springs to Williamsville 30 years before. The Ralph Plumb mentioned—former Town of Collins supervisor, state assemblyman, and Erie County sheriff—is the same Ralph Plumb who had sued Bennett in 1824 for loss of merchandise in a shipwreck.

[32] Erie County officeholders were nearly 100 percent Whigs at the time. The Whigs were of the same party as the new president of the United States, Buffalo's Millard Fillmore. Following the approaching demise of the Whig Party, brought about in large part by Fillmore's signing of the highly divisive Fugitive Slave Act into law, Bennett would ally himself with the new Republican Party.

[33] The Col. Plumb referred to is Joseph H. Plumb, eldest son of Ralph Plumb, and a colonel in the 169th Regiment of New York

# Joseph Bennett

Charles C. Severance was nominated and subsequently elected for the 1851 term (terms at that time being for one year only).

During the month following Severance's nomination, October 1850, Bennett's growing political connections paid off for his family in the person of his 22-year-old son Seymour. Bennett was asked early that month by former Buffalo mayor William Ketchum, presently serving as Collector of the Port in Buffalo, if he "had a son who would like to be appointed one of the Inspectors of Customs in the Custom House department of Buffalo." Patronage was rife, and acceptable—Ketchum himself held his job because of his friendship with President Fillmore—and Bennett was not about to let such an opportunity pass. He quickly assured the former mayor that he indeed had such a son, and by the end of the month young Seymour was at work in his new post.

But if Joseph Bennett had escaped being sentenced to Albany once, he would not escape it a second time. The following September he was nominated as his party's candidate for the 1852 term. He would be elected in November "by a very strong vote," and would proceed to Albany as one of Erie County's four assemblymen.

Throughout this busy period of his life, when he had served as a construction contractor, railroad appraiser, town supervisor, member of the penitentiary board, and now potentially as a state officeholder—one of Joseph Bennett's ongoing duties had been to investigate deaths as a county coroner. "During the last six years," he related, "that I have held the office of Coroner have been called upon to hold many inquests, all of fatal and sad

---

State militia. He would later serve several terms as Town of Collins supervisor, and two terms as assemblyman. Charles C. Severance had practiced law in Springville since 1833. He had served several terms as Town of Concord supervisor and already one term as assemblyman. Elected Justice of the Peace in 1840, he would hold that post almost continuously for decades.

events, some more than others (strikingly so). I will state only one case."

The case arose between his nomination to the assembly and his election.

"On the 26th day of October, 1851," he explained, "(on Sunday) was notified that a body was found in Hamburgh on the lake shore, opposite the high banks."

This would likely be between Eighteen-Mile Creek and Clifton Heights in today's Lake View.

"About noon," he continued,

> when I first saw the body it was laying on the beach by the side of a skiff that was partly drawn out of the water. The night before was a cold, dark, stormy night. The man did not look like a dead man. I think if proper measures had been taken when first found early in the morning the man could have been saved. I found upon the body a bunch of keys, and a bill of sale of some goods. The next morning I went to Buffalo. By the aid of the bill of sale, went to a business house, asked the proprietor, if he knew anything of this paper. Why yes, and how in the world did you come by it. I then showed him the bunch of keys. He looked at me with astonishment. Those are our keys, and have been anxiously waiting for them all morning. Please do explain, I fear there is something wrong. I evaded answering but asked him where the keys were kept and who should have them. He said, Our man Thos. Stamp always took charge of the premises at night, and every Saturday night after business hours went to his family in Canada. (What way does he go?) Sometimes in his little skiff, sometime by ferry. I then told him that Mr. Stamp was dead, that I had held an inquest the day before, that the body was cared for, that I was waiting to find friends if possible, and they are found.

Thomas Stamp had ventured out upon Lake Erie on a night when he should probably have taken the ferry. Mr. Stamp, concluded Bennett, "was evidently out all night and lost, came on shore 11 miles from Buffalo evidently, overworked, cold, wet, and exhausted."

The following month, the county coroner, by now also assemblyman-elect, reported another incident, albeit non-tragic. "In November, 1851," he wrote,

> some 200 blb. flour came on shore from an unknown vessel. I took the flour in charge by virtue of my office as Coroner, gathered the flour from along the shore into two places, in a day or two. The underwriter, Capt. Dorr of Buffalo, requested me to dispose of the flour the best I could and report to him, which I did to his satisfaction.

Following this entry he noted, "Am now making preparations for leaving home for Albany."

♣

On Saturday January 3, 1852, Bennett, in company with fellow legislator and former Town of Amherst supervisor Jasper B. Youngs, climbed aboard the train for Albany.

"Arrived in Albany in the evening," he related. "On Monday following," he continued,

> the usual caucusing for Speaker, Clerks, Sergeant-at-Arms and other officers of the Assembly, and Whig nominations made. On Tuesday, temporary organization. Members took the oath of office and elected officers, permanently organized and received the governor's message. Myself and friend took board at 128 State Street with Miss Shaw. On Wednesday (7th), cast lots or drew our seats and adjourned.
>
> Met next day and adjourned until next Monday, no committees yet.

On his first Sunday in Albany he attended Dr. Luther Beecher's Baptist church. Beecher was a cousin of preacher and abolitionist Henry Ward Beecher and of Henry's sister, Harriet Beecher Stowe, author of the explosive antislavery novel *Uncle Tom's Cabin*, recently serialized and about to be published as a book.

# Erie County Citizen

Despite Bennett's comfort level with the Whig governor—Washington Hunt, of Lockport—Albany proved to be an agony for him. He appeared to enjoy a party he attended on February 3 at the governor's mansion, but found his duties on the assembly floor tedious in the extreme. "Things are moving terribly slow in the legislature," he recorded.

> The great, and most exciting question, is temperance. A prohibitory bill before the Assembly is being discussed with great enthusiasm. Petitions are coming in with thousands of names praying for the Main [sic] Law, as it is termed.[34]   Rolls of petitions wound around polls [sic], brought in upon the shoulders of two men. Nearly all the Democrats are opposed to the bill, all the advocates are from the Whigs. I think the efforts in behalf of temperance will fail for the present. But it is God's cause and will eventually succeed.

He must have hit it off with the governor at the previous gathering (they may in fact have been acquainted already), because a couple of days later he and the governor together attended the public examinations at the Albany State Normal School, the first college for teachers in New York State, founded in 1844.[35]  He and Governor Hunt found themselves seated in the "audience room" on the third floor of the school's new building, where they were about to be caught up in more than a public examination of future teachers.

"Gov. Hunt and myself," he recalled,

> were sitting on a bench together, the audience being very large. All at once, about the middle of the exer-

---

[34] "Maine Law" refers to Maine's total ban, in 1851, on the manufacture and sale of liquor. Maine was a leader in the cause of temperance, which would become a dominant theme of national political discourse for decades. The Maine Law remained in effect to some extent until the repeal of National Prohibition in 1933.

[35] The school was the forerunner of the State University of New York at Albany.

cise, the floor settled (*with a loud noise*) about 4 inches in the center of the room. Women screamed and a general rush for the stairs, only the one place of escape. A man mounted the rostrum, and with a loud voice said, For *God's* sake don't rush for the stairs, there is no danger, the floor is arched and cannot fall. The panic being a little quieted, about one half of the people passed down stairs and out. Gov. Hunt and myself stayed. In about half an hour later, another settle, before the close of the exercise. The floor settled again, over 2 inches. I concluded duty demanded my attention in another direction and left.

It is unknown whether the governor, too, heard the call of duty from beyond the building.

Later this same week, Joseph, having been appointed to the committee on prisons, journeyed with committee members to Ossining to visit and report on conditions at Sing Sing state prison. The committee apparently was satisfied with what they observed, since, according to Joseph, the official report stated "prison and management all right."

"Such examinations and reports," he commented, "are all *bosh.*"

A few days later, on February 11, he reported meeting with a joint committee of the assembly and senate on the assessment of taxes. "No results," he said.

"No subject in our internal and important relations," he concluded, "more difficult to adjust by legislation than the tax sistem [*sic*]."

Despite the trips, social gatherings, long-winded speeches, and meetings without results, it appears that Assemblyman Bennett did attempt to accomplish something for his region while in Albany.

# Erie County Citizen

"I presented and assisted in carrying through a number of bills in the interest of Buffalo," he declared, "one in relation to the International Bridge at Black Rock."[36]

In an uncharacteristic slap at a fellow lawmaker, he continued, in reference to Erie County assemblyman and future congressman Israel T. Hatch: "Mr. I.T. Hatch, the member from Buffalo, was so deeply engaged and absorbed in Canal matters that he would not attend to local matters in the interest of his constituents even."

It is perhaps not surprising that the source of Joseph's pique was a Democrat.

On February 21 a special train took the entire state government and guests to Troy for a traditional event: a Washington's Birthday banquet hosted by the city government. Not so wrapped up in the interests of Buffalo that he could not enjoy a party, Bennett pronounced the banquet "a splendid affair."

On March 4, 1852, Assemblyman Bennett received surprising news from home—he had once again been elected supervisor of the Town of Evans. "Very unexpected to me," he commented. It is not known if this news caused the illness that he soon suffered, but he was in fact forced to take to his bed for the next three days, nursed by his young ward and future physician, Thaddeus Seeley, who was attending school in Schenectady. Following his recovery and a quick trip

---

[36] Bennett seems to be referring to a scheme to construct a bridge across the upper Niagara River (i.e., the portion between Buffalo and the Falls), which did not occur until 1873 when the International Railroad Bridge was opened. A suspension bridge had been in service across the lower river (i.e., the portion between the Falls and Lake Ontario) since 1848. It carried both pedestrian and carriage traffic across the gorge, swaying and dipping frighteningly, but without failure or accident. In 1851, the year before Bennett came to Albany, John A. Roebling, the future builder of the Brooklyn Bridge, had been awarded a contract to construct a railway suspension bridge over the lower river, and began construction in September 1852. The first locomotive crossed this solid bridge in 1855.

home he took up his legislative duties again until April 17, when the legislature adjourned (at 5:30 AM, following an all-night session). He was home by April 19.[37]

His one-sentence pronouncement on his Albany experience: "I have a very poor opinion of so much legislation."

---

[37] Bennett's journal says that the legislature adjourned in March. Internal evidence suggests he meant April.

# 6

# IN THE SHADOW OF WAR

As a possible sign that Joseph was just happy to be home, and perhaps too busy to write, he recorded little of the remainder of 1852. Not that 1852 was not important, because it was—for the town, as well as for Bennett personally. The railroad from Erie, Pennsylvania, to Albany and New York now passed within a mile of Evans Center, and the future of the community looked considerably brighter. Unfortunately for Evans Center, however, a clump of three or four houses to the east lay closer to the railroad, and it is this community that would, as Angola, soon eclipse Evans Center in growth and prosperity.

The 48-year old town supervisor appears to have occupied himself that summer in the things he liked to do. "28th of June," he wrote, "my wife and myself went to Buffalo in the afternoon, in a very small metalic [sic] life boat and back in the evening in [railroad] cars."

On July 3 he attended an Independence Day celebration at Sturgeon Point. "I served by *appointment*" he noted, "as president of the day."

On October 5 he was elected chairman of the Erie County Board of Supervisors, and was shortly thereafter reelected county coroner. He notes also at this time that he was teaching Sabbath school every Sunday.

His plate was, as usual, quite full.

# Joseph Bennett

On March 7, 1853, Mary's remaining parent, Michael Roat, died in the home of Aaron Salisbury, at the age of 89. Declared Joseph, remembering both of Mary's parents, "Our heavenly Father enabled them to live to a good old age."

Margaret and Michael Roat, formerly of New Jersey, are buried in the Pioneer Cemetery at Evans Center.

As continuing bearer of the title "County Coroner," Joseph never knew what a day might bring. "I am very frequently called upon to hold inquests," he wrote,

> where cause of death is not known or where there might be any suspision [sic] of crime or where unknown bodies are found in any locality without friends.

> On the 21st day of April 1853, I was notified that Mr. Stephen Parks was found on his premises in the Town of Evans, dead with his throat cut. I held an inquest. Verdict of jury, "Cut his own throat" with a razor, caused by mental derangement.

"On the 27th day of April," he continued,

> Mr. Webber (a member of our church), a very nice man, was found dead in a small brook near his house. I being a coroner, was notified at once. Made a thorough examination, found he was subject to epilepsy, or falling sickness fits, would frequently and suddenly, fall insensibly. It was evident he fell into the water, and drowned.

> I concluded not to hold an inquest. The remains were buried on the 29th in cemetery at Evans.

♧

Beginning in the 1830s, farsighted men had seen that Buffalo, by virtue of its location, was destined to become one of the growing nation's most important transportation hubs. The canal had been the first step to the realization of that vision, but it was the advance of the railroads that had truly made the vision a reality. One of the least known but most efficacious of the railroad visionar-

# In the Shadow of War

ies had been William Wallace, the driving force behind nearly every rail line that had come into the city, beginning with the Buffalo and Attica line that had opened in January 1843, and that had made possible rail travel from Albany to Buffalo. Wallace had been chief engineer of the Buffalo and State Line, and of the extension of the Buffalo and Attica road to Hornellsville (present-day Hornell), in Steuben County. Before his death in 1887 he would be instrumental in cementing Buffalo further into the thickening network of iron rails that was binding all sections of the young nation ever more tightly together.

But in 1853 Wallace was bent on linking Buffalo to the west by the most direct of routes—across lower Ontario. He had already projected and surveyed the Buffalo, Brantford and Goderich line, which would link Buffalo to Goderich, on the Ontario shore of Lake Huron, via Brantford, lying about 20 miles west of Hamilton. He would serve as Chief Engineer for construction of the line, a project already under way in places, but of which large sections remained unbegun. Joseph Bennett wanted a piece of this construction, and, when he heard of an upcoming bidding session in Brantford, he contacted Wallace and made arrangements to attend the session in company with the Chief Engineer. The bidding session, expected to last several days, promised to be heavily attended. The two men were to travel together in Wallace's carriage, but since Wallace could not leave as early as Bennett, he turned over his team and carriage to the Evans man, with a promise to catch up with him by train at Niagara Falls. They would continue the overnight trip together.

Joseph, a veteran bidder and builder, had high hopes of getting a lucrative piece of work in Canada. He was unprepared for the disappointment about to come his way.

"The 11th of May," he recounted,

left Buffalo in a carriage belonging to Mr. Wallace, engineer of the Buffalo and Brantford R.R. . . . Mr.

# Joseph Bennett

Wallace waited in Buffalo on business, and came on the noon train, and overtook me at Niagara Falls. From there to Lewiston in carriage, then shipped the horses and carriage to Hamilton in steam boat, from Hamilton to Brantford in carriage, arrived in Brantford on the morning of the 12th.

Here I am looking for a job of work on the R.R. The commissioners meet this week to receive proposals, and will continue in session for a number of days. I spent a number of days examining the rout [sic]. On the 16th handed in my tender for 40 miles of work. There were a large number of men that sent in their proposals. Some were much higher than mine, the most of them were lower. A company in Brantford took the contract, but they can never do the work at the price.

One of the commissioners or directors came from Brantford in company with me to Niagara, and in conversation said, the contract was taken very low. He thought my proposals very fair.

But Joseph appears to have learned from the plank road project that not taking a job is preferable to taking one that loses money. His conclusion: "Came home without a job, had rather be idle than work for nothing."

He used his "idle" time that spring to build a carriage house on his property.

♣

Joseph Bennett, one of whose first purchases when setting up housekeeping as a young man had been a half barrel of whiskey, was by now a dedicated temperance advocate. He had joined a number of temperance organizations over the years, most recently the Union of Temperance. He seems, however, to have been accepting of those who did not share his views. Writing of his presiding over an Independence Day temperance celebration at Sturgeon Point in 1853—a doubtless stern assembly, under the Union of Temperance banner—he somewhat

# In the Shadow of War

impishly noted that an "Anti-Temperance" rally had taken place the same day at Jerusalem Corners, "with lots of whisky fun."

♣

Since the 1700s and before, engineers had been interested in how air could be delivered to a man under water for a long enough period that he could do useful work below the surface. Various forms of protection and air delivery had been tried, beginning with iron diving bells, followed by suiting the diver in leather, metallic, and later rubber "armor," supplying air first via a simple bellows and passing, during the nineteenth century, on to the piston pump and pressurized (surface) tank. Methods of releasing spent air varied, but were not yet dependable.

By 1853, divers were using flexible rubberized suits, the vulcanization process having been perfected by Charles Goodyear a few years previous. Both glass and metallic headgear were in use. Since the problems of dependable delivery and exhaust of air and pressure equalization had not been totally solved, diving remained a hazardous occupation.

On Wednesday July 20, a novice diver named William McDonald (or McDonnell) was under water off the mouth of Cattaraugus Creek, exploring what remained of the wreckage of the celebrated steamboat *Erie*. In August 1841 the *Erie* had caught fire and gone down with 200 passengers, largely German and Swiss immigrants. The disaster had been caused by a crew of careless painters, en route from Buffalo to Erie, Pennsylvania, who had stowed their turpentine and paints downwind of the ship's two spark-belching stacks. The *Erie*, which had borne valuable cargo in addition to passengers, had lately been lifted from the lake bottom by celebrated diver and salvager John Green, and towed to Buffalo, but remnants of the wreckage remained in place.

McDonald, apparently one of Green's divers, was directed to inspect the wreckage remaining off Cattaraugus

# Joseph Bennett

Creek. Since, prior to the raising of the *Erie* from 66 feet of water, dives of greater than 45 feet had been considered extremely dangerous, it seems odd that a novice diver would have been given this task.

Sometime during McDonald's second descent to the bottom, his crew on the surface lost contact with him, and, following strenuous efforts, proved unable to raise him. He had evidently become entangled in the wreck, and was finally given up for lost. The news was carried to Green.

On Sunday July 24, Green and another diver descended to the wreck, found the body, and brought it to the surface. The head was swollen, and blood had been forced from the mouth and ears. Coroner Bennett was summoned. Following the coroner's inquest, Bennett pronounced that the "deceased came to his death from apoplexy, caused by the pressure of the atmosphere and in consequence of having to breathe the same air several times over."[38]

Since even coroners have their private lives, Coroner Bennett returned quickly to his own, the unfortunate diver forgotten. "Am engaged in farming during the summer," he reported. Then: "In October attended the County Fair. Took two squashes weighing 224 lbs. and 226 lbs each. Sold one for $11.00, the other for $12.50, and the premium $1.00."

At this point Bennett's journal begins to chronicle an appalling list—appalling at least to us—of young peoples' deaths, all of persons close to him.

November 30, 1854: Eliza Butler, the 32-year-old daughter of O.H. Dibble, niece of Joseph's wife Mary, a "talented and beautiful woman." January 8, 1855: Eliza Salisbury, 18-year-old daughter of Judge Aaron Salisbury, also Mary's niece, dead of consumption (i.e., pulmonary tuberculosis). December 22, 1856: Mary Salis-

---

[38] *Buffalo Daily Courier*, July 27, 1853.

bury, another daughter of Aaron and niece of Mary Bennett, 25 years old, also dead of consumption. A "superior young lady," remarked Joseph. March 29, 1857: Emma Sweetland, another Salisbury daughter, 31 years old, the wife of George Sweetland, Jr. "The third daughter that has died within the last two years," remarked Joseph. "All beautiful young ladies, sad, how sad."

Tragedy seemed loathe, for a time, to depart this little corner of western New York. In July 1855, an early-morning fire broke out in the Town of Brant home of 54-year old farmer James Thompson. Having succeeded in escaping the burning house with most of his large family, Thompson returned to rescue his three daughters (ages 28, 13, and 11) and two grandchildren (ages 4 and 2), who had not yet gotten out. All, including Thompson, were lost. Suspicion of arson fell upon the estranged husband of the eldest daughter, father of the two small children.[39]

"I summoned a jury of inquest," wrote Joseph,

> and commenced an examination. Not being able to get any clue to the origin of the fire, supposed it to be an accident. As there were some suspicion of wrong, among the inhabitants, I adjourned the inquest, three days. During the adjournment Dr. [Luther] Buxton and others, made thorough investigation but could elicit no crime. On the adjourned day, the Coroners Jury convened. No additional testimony. Verdict of jury, "Cause of fire unknown."

It was during these years that the Bennetts' children began leaving the nest. Their eldest daughter Jane was the first married—to Seth Henry Barrell, in May 1853. She and her husband would soon move to tiny Amboy, Illinois, 90 miles west of Chicago. In January 1855, Seymour married Susan Barton in New York City.

---

[39] Description taken from *Buffalo Morning Express*, July 17, 1855. The account differs in some particulars from Bennett's.

# Joseph Bennett

The 52-year old former supervisor and state assemblyman still had three children at home, and, with one of them, was getting back to farm life. In September 1855, with his 20-year-old son Judson, he was taking large hemlocks down—at last able to realize a profit on timber, with local roads finally suitable for moving heavy loads. He estimated that he and Judson that month had sawed and transported (via lake vessel) to Buffalo between 100,000 and 200,000 board feet of lumber, enough to build several houses. What he received in payment is unknown, but he reported his expenses as $2.00 per thousand for sawing and $1.50 per thousand for freight.

The following April, he recorded the dedication of the new Baptist meeting house. "Our church is a nice little pleasant well furnished church for a country place," he said. "Our church members number 125, besides a good society of Baptists in sentiment."

In August, 25-year-old daughter Jane began packing to join her new husband in Amboy. On the 26th, she took a steamboat from Buffalo for the five-day trip to Chicago, with a lady friend and Elder Danforth of the church. Henry had been in Amboy for the previous three months preparing a home. "I do not find any pleasure in giving up my children," wrote Joseph, "for other and new interests."

By October 1857, he and Mary had decided they now had sufficient reason to take another trip west, and did so, traveling this time by train. They visited Joseph's 47-year-old sister Sarah, who had married a Baptist minister named Jacob Price and remained in "the west," namely, Michigan. Jacob and Sarah had seven children. The Bennetts then went to New Buffalo, Michigan, where, with Joseph's 50-year-old brother Alonzo, they visited the graves of Joseph's parents, Samuel and Sally Bennett.

"Oh what a solemn visit," recalled Bennett,

shall never forget the crushing emotions. While I stood intently viewing the mounds, recollections of the past came rolling up before me. Their toils and untiring devotion, in sickness, in health, in prosperity and adversity alike. Their all, their everything sacrificed to their numerous children, all grew to manhood and womanhood, not a moral blemish upon one of them. I now feel that I appreciate their wonderful goodness and devotion. As I stood leaning over the graves, the thought arose, are you dear father and mother our guiding star still?

I bid farewell to this solemn place and tore myself away.

From New Buffalo they proceeded to Amboy, Illinois, where they found Jane "very comfortably situated." Following a two-week stay with Jane, during which time they roamed as far as they could over the Illinois prairies, they turned homeward via South Bend, where Joseph's sister, 52-year-old Rhoda Grannis, made her home with her husband John and several children. "Found them all well situated," reported Joseph. "This is a fine new country. We arrived at home on the 6th of November, and have had a very pleasant journey."

Surprisingly, Bennett made no journal entries for 1858, dismissing the entire year with, "Time has rolled on for the last year very monotinous [sic] with the ordinary casulties [sic]."

On March 21, 1859, he recorded that his 26-year-old daughter Henrietta had "brought home from Buffalo" little Lizzie Butler, about 7 years old. Lizzie was the granddaughter of O.H. Dibble and daughter of Eliza Dibble Butler, who had died nearly five years previous—"a little motherless niece and cousin of our children," he noted. It is unknown with whom she had been living in Buffalo, but Bennett clearly regarded her present status as temporary. "We expect," he commented, "the little girl will live with us in the future."

Seymour, still working at the Port of Buffalo, owned a sailboat that Bennett was fond of taking out whenever possible. It was kept sometimes in Evans and sometimes

# Joseph Bennett

in Buffalo, train transport between the two places being dependable enough that one-way boat trips were easily made. Same-day round trips were sometimes also possible. "Often sail to Buffalo and back with my wife and daughters [Henrietta and 22-year-old Josephine]," he declared.

> We are all passionately fond of sailing, and delight in taking parties sailing. I hardly ever saw or knew a person so passionately fond of sailing as Judge Salisbury. Often when we leave home for Buffalo, the judge (living a mile or two towards Buffalo, on the shore) seeing us coming would runn [sic] to the house and say, Wife, don't you want something from Buffalo. She would laugh and he would signal us. We take him in.

Whether Bennett sought out responsibility or whether it sought him, against the background of a large and threatening national disturbance he was thrust back into the fray. In November 1859 the 56-year-old former assemblyman, supervisor, chairman of the Board of Supervisors, and coroner was elected one of three Superintendents of the Poor for Erie County. On January 1, 1860, he entered upon the duties of his office, meeting with his two new colleagues on that date. The superintendents' first order of business proved to be establishment of staff positions to run the department and, in particular, the poorhouse. They named a Principal Keeper, Matrons, Insane Keepers, Physicians, and a few lower positions. Importantly, they elected one of their own Clerk of the Board. This unfortunate superintendent was expected to virtually live on or near the poorhouse premises, and to be on call around the clock. The other two superintendents needed only to attend meetings as necessary.

Bennett seems to have underestimated the demands of his new position. He was, for example, shocked by the immediate barrage of petitions for jobs and contracts.

# In the Shadow of War

"The amount of pressure brought to bear for the appointment to the different positions," he wrote, "is astonishing. (Then for supplies.) The butcher, grocer, merchant, druggist, and all others wishing to furnish from their special trade." But he—and presumably his fellow guardians of the government purse—had had decades of experience in handling people and in making decisions. "We shall," he declared, "make no changes at present."

He and his associates were good to their word. No new appointment was made until the end of September, when Dr. Frederick F. Hoyer of Tonawanda was named Physician to the Poorhouse.

The Bennetts' daughter Jane, who would never bear children, spent the summer and fall in the Town of Evans with her mother and her increasingly busy father. In October 1860, as she was preparing to leave for her Illinois home, her father remarked on the improvement he had noted in her health: "The western country seems to agree with her very much." He continued, as many fathers might: "We always feel sad, very sad, when our children leave home, the old homestead, for their new relations and home. But such is life, always has been, and always will be."

One of Bennett's new duties as Superintendent of the Poor was the escorting of persons judged insane, but curable, to the State Lunatic Asylum at Utica. "I took an insane man by the name of Taft, a Quaker," related Bennett,

> to the Insane Asylum at Utica. On the way, in the cars, before making Utica, he formed a wonderful attachment to a lady passenger. It was with much difficulty that I could separate him from her (at Utica). She manifested a sympathy for him, and said she would go to the asylum with me, if she had time.

Joseph did not record whether the lady actually found the time to accompany her new friend.

123

# Joseph Bennett

♣

In his journal Bennett notes an event that occurred in that fateful election month of November 1860, an event in which many lives were lost: the November 24 wreck, in the Town of Evans, of the 198-foot propeller *Dacotah*, in one of the most powerful storms of the decade, one that featured gale-force southwest winds and blinding snow.[40] The Chicago-bound vessel, which had departed Buffalo earlier in the day, was carrying not only a valuable cargo of copper ingots, but also the crew of the propeller *Marquette*, who were hitching a ride home after their vessel had been laid up for the season. The *Dacotah*, running into the teeth of an increasingly unmanageable storm, was apparently steering for shelter in Lake Bay off the Town of Evans when, sometime after dark, it struck a rock and its hull was opened. The ship began to break up and founder as it careened through the mountainous waves toward shore. The 34 men aboard appear to have ridden the splintered upper works and a lifeboat through the surf, soaked through by the icy water, with many apparently reaching shore alive.[41] Exhausted, however, and suffering from exposure, they could move no farther. Hearing cries in the darkness, Joseph, Mary, and Judson got dressed, grabbed a lantern, and pushed out into the wind and blinding snow to investigate. They saw nothing and could hear nothing but the fierce wind. Mary remained so sure that she had heard cries that, at first light, she sent Judson to investigate, and everything quickly became apparent. The wreck, cargo, and bodies of the men, dead from exposure, were strewn for hundreds of yards along the snow-covered beach. Two feet of snow had fallen during the night.[42]

---

[40] "Propeller" was the common name for a steam-driven vessel with a propeller as opposed to paddle-wheels.
[41] Bennett's account says 34 men aboard. Other accounts say 24.
[42] Account based on *Buffalo Morning Express*, November 28, 1860.

# In the Shadow of War

"Not a person saved," said Bennett, "to tell the story."

♣

Like many others, Bennett's mind must have been on the national plight as 1860 turned to 1861, but his duties on the Poor Board kept him fully occupied. As he began his second year of service on the board, he had the misfortune of being elected Clerk, an event that promised a much increased activity level over the previous year. Since he would now be on call around the clock, he moved in with his son Seymour, who, with his wife and young daughter, lived in the city.[43]

Others in the family did what they could to relieve his burden. In January, his youngest daughter Josephine, for example, filled in as schoolteacher at the poorhouse until the hired teacher could get there.

"Am now constantly in Buffalo," he reported, "during the week attending to all requirements, purchasing supplies for poor house, auditing county and city accounts, and claims against the two departments."

In February, however, something memorable happened, something that made it worthwhile to be in Buffalo instead of at home in Evans. "On the 16th of February," he recalled, "the President of the United States (Elect) arrived in Buffalo on his way to Washington. The gathering of the people was immense, the excitement great, times perilous."

"The rebels," he added, in an entry obviously made later, "intended to entrap Mr. Lincoln on his way to Washington but were foiled."[44]

His notation on the opening act of the unfolding tragedy followed: "On the 14th of April Fort Sumpter [sic] sur-

---

[43] Susan Isabella ("Belle") Bennett had been born January 8, 1858.

[44] This doubtless refers to the plot to assassinate Lincoln as he passed through a seethingly hostile Baltimore en route to Washington. The plot was foiled by Detective Allan Pinkerton, who spirited the president-elect through Baltimore in disguise and by night.

rendered to the rebel forces after 36 hours of terrible bombardment."

♧

Buffalo was not slow to respond to the new president's call for volunteers. "On the 3rd of May," reported Joseph,

> a regiment of Volunteers left Buffalo for Washington, the first regiment from Erie County, and were escorted to the depot by the celebrated Home Guards amid great cheering and enthusiasm. Ex President Filmore [*sic*], Captain of the Home Guards, Ex Postmaster General Judge Hall, . . . judges, merchants, bank men, all of high standing, were the rank and file of the company. I think the only company ever organized in America as Home Guards, commanded by a President of the United States, and officered by his cabinet.

Joseph was 57 years old when Sumter fell, and he was probably not tempted to volunteer. Besides, he had an important job to do in Erie County, New York. "I am constantly engaged," he declared, "attending Poor Department." He was in complete sympathy with the Union cause, having by now joined, or at least become sympathetic to, the new Republican Party.

Apart from uneasiness at the outbreak of hostilities, and the need to supply manpower to the army, western New York life in this summer of 1861 was not terribly affected by the storm brewing only 400 miles away. As the two novice armies probed each other, feeling one another tentatively before their sudden death embrace on the banks of a stream called Bull Run, those at home could only wait for the news and live life as it had been lived.

"On the 26th [of June]," wrote Joseph, "Etta [Henrietta] and Josephine and myself went to Grand Island on a visit to Mr. John Nice."

# In the Shadow of War

Nice, a German immigrant, was one of Bennett's fellow Superintendents of the Poor, having been elected with him in 1860. He had been the first supervisor of the new Town of Grand Island, and remained one of the island's most active citizens. In future years he would serve two terms in the state assembly, and would be a delegate to the Republican National Convention in 1880.

"Mr. Nice took us," continued Joseph,

> with his family and friends (in his tug) around the head of the island to Falkenwood, an elaborate supper at midnight, enjoyed the festivities of the occasion, during the whole night.[45] Arrived at Mr. Nice's home next morning at sunrise.

On July 4, Bennett noted that war excitement was intense, meetings were being called, speeches being made, and men enlisting. But five days later he made a notation of a different kind: "July 9th, Judge Salisbury died this evening, very suddenly while sitting in his chair. Dropsey [i.e., congestive heart failure] the cause of his death."

"For more than forty years," he continued

> have been intimately acquainted with him, part of that time have been engaged in business together. He was a man of unusual strength of intellect and character. He raised a family of eight children of more than ordinary brilliancy of character.

---

[45] "Falkenwood" was actually Falconwood, a summer resort constructed on the southwest shore of Grand Island by Lewis F. Allen, and opened in 1859. Allen, uncle of Grover Cleveland, in 1833 had joined with some Boston men in purchasing 16,000 acres of timbered land on the island. They erected what was thought to be the largest steam sawmill in the world and began to transport white oak lumber, via the canal, to shipyards in New York and Boston. Allen Street in Buffalo is named for Lewis F. Allen. Nice's ownership of a tug was likely due to his involvement in the Grand Island timber business.

# Joseph Bennett

On July 22, he learned of the previous day's carnage—and astonishing rout of Union troops—at Manassas, Virginia.

♣

The Kingdom of the Poor of Erie County over which Bennett reigned was dismal indeed.

The poor of Bennett's times were divided into two classes: the permanent poor, supported year round at the public expense, and the temporary poor, who received assistance part of the year, usually in autumn and winter. A large percentage of the permanent poor—housed in the poorhouse, or almshouse—had achieved their status, it was widely acknowledged, through "excessive use of ardent spirits."

With respect to the permanent poor, it was the job of the superintendents to prescribe rules for the governance of the institution, to set dietary standards, and to procure all necessary food and supplies. In regard to the temporary poor, some towns had established small budgets that they administered themselves.

Since the early 1850s, the Erie County poorhouse had been located on the Williamsville Road, on the present site of the State University South Campus. The poorhouse and adjoining insane asylum were sited on a 153-acre working farm. A fire in February 1855 had made reconstruction of the poorhouse necessary. The fire was fortuitous, however, in that it made possible certain sanitary improvements, such as the better handling of sewage.

In 1857, the Erie County poorhouse had been inspected by the state. The inspecting team had reported that the number of inmates at the joint facility was 225, of which 150 were males and 75 females.[46] Those who

---

[46] The *average* number of inmates was put at 300. The lower number prevailing in 1857 was possibly due to a cholera outbreak that had occurred at the facility just prior to the 1855 fire. The

were able were expected to work on the farm or about the house. Although there were 34 wards, "well warmed and partially ventilated," it was reported that as many as 30 inmates were found lodged in a single ward. The inmates—almost all of whom were "of foreign birth"—were cared for by six keepers, three male and three female. A teacher was supplied for resident children, usually numbering about 45, but at the time of the inspection, 75. Children reaching the age of 16 were "bound out" of the facility by the superintendents, possibly into indenture. A physician, paid $400 per year, visited the inmates twice a week. Despite the improvements in sanitation following the 1855 fire, no arrangements existed for bathing. At this time there were 71 "lunatics" among the inmates, 26 males and 45 females.[47] Twelve of these had already been treated at the Utica Asylum, and were presumably diagnosed as incurable. At the time of the inspection the poorhouse sheltered 11 "idiots," and three blind persons. The building was pronounced by the inspectors to be "in a clean and orderly condition."

During 1856-57, the institution had seen 34 births and 83 deaths.

The large insane asylum adjoining the poorhouse had 72 cells. At the time of the 1857 inspection, only one inmate was confined day and night, with the rest allowed to roam the halls and yards, and to be confined only at night. Recalcitrant inmates were commonly restrained by shackling and handcuffing in a chair. The insane received the same medical attention as the paupers, but could be discharged by the superintendents only on the advice of the physician. In 1857 their care had been pronounced by the inspection team to be "good," and the facility "cleanly and well kept."

---

report on the 1857 investigation may be found at http://www.poorhousestory.com/ERIE.htm.

[47] These unfortunates are described as subjects of the poorhouse inspection, but they may have resided in the insane asylum.

# Joseph Bennett

On September 19, 1861, another fire struck the Erie County poorhouse, leaving—according to Bennett, who by this time lived on the premises—only a small portion of the building usable. With winter coming, and no place to send the inmates, county government found itself in a serious predicament.

"We were," recalled Superintendent Bennett, "without shelter for 3[00] or 400 inmates. All dissabled [sic] ones we sent around to different assylums [sic]. Rappidly [sic] made shanties for healthiest ones." The county Board of Supervisors immediately passed a resolution authorizing the Committee on Fiscal Affairs to borrow $12,000 for the reconstruction of the poorhouse, and directing the Superintendents of the Poor to get the work started.

"I being the resident Superintendent and Clerk of the Board," explained Joseph, "had nearly all the work to do. We put on a large force of men and pushed the work as rapidly as possible."

Superintendent Bennett's abilities in construction management do not seem to have been widely known, judging from the *Buffalo Daily Courier* of October 8, 1861, which fretted editorially that no "competent person [had] been employed to make any plan," and expressed disbelief in the competence of the superintendents to carry on a work of this importance.

"They are not practical builders," argued the editor,

> they have no experience in either construction or managing institutions of this kind . . . The excuse for this haste is the immediate necessity of the completion of the building, but this is no reason for voting $12,000 of County Bonds into the hands of three inexperienced men without supervision or contract of any sort.[48]

The editorial must have stung Joseph because he replied in a published letter—carefully tinged with sarcasm—the following day:

---

[48] *Buffalo Daily Courier*, October 8, 1861.

# In the Shadow of War

Very dear sir: I saw in your paper last evening an article headed The Rebuilding of the Erie County Poor House, in which I am happy to discover, you feel a deep interest and desire to guard the county against fraud, as every large tax-payer should. I do therefore invite you to call at this office as early as possible, and examine the plan and specification of the building, which has been made with much care and labor. It was exhibited to the Board of Supervisors in the early part of last week; it has also been exhibited to many first-class builders, and has their approval. No doubt you may suggest some important improvements, which will be thankfully received. The Superintendents intend to appoint some competent builders to superintend the construction of the building, "this afternoon." I hope you will not fail to call and give the necessary information and instruction. Your obedient servant, Joseph Bennett, Superintendent of Poor[49]

Not to be outdone in sarcasm, but seeming to flee the field, the editor replied below Bennett's letter:

We have great pleasure in giving our readers an opportunity to peruse this letter, not only because it is interesting as a literary production, but because it contains valuable information . . . They want to spend the $12,000 at their own discretion, and if this should not prove to be sufficient to complete the building, they can ask the dear, good Board of Supervisors for more . . . If Mr. Bennett proves to be as sharp in looking after the interests of the county as he tries to be with his pen, we shall have some confidence that he will spend the $12,000 judiciously.[50]

The county supervisors and the other two superintendents, however, evidently knew what they had in Joseph Bennett, for in January 1862, Bennett was again

---

[49] *Buffalo Daily Courier*, October 9, 1861.
[50] Ibid.

elected Clerk of the Board, apparently with the under-standing that he would continue to supervise the re-building of the poorhouse. The inmates must have passed the entire winter in temporary housing, since Bennett reports that he had to attend to the rebuilding of the structure every day throughout that period.

As spring broke, however, his construction oversight obligations tailed off and he resumed some of his former duties, such as conducting insane patients to Utica, or bringing them back from there. In May 1862 he recorded a trip from Utica with a female patient who, after two years in the Utica Asylum, had been pronounced incur-able and who for that reason was being remanded to Erie County.

♣

The war continued as a worrisome backdrop to life. These were the days of bloody fighting on the Peninsula east of Richmond, yet—unknown to all—the coming slaughter on the banks of Antietam Creek and the filling of the Rappahannock with rafts of Union corpses in De-cember would dwarf these early-summer losses.

As defeat after defeat befell Union armies that sum-mer, the president grew increasingly disenchanted with his general, George B. McClellan. But not only new mili-tary leadership seemed called for. More men were needed. A call for 300,000 more volunteers went out that summer, with a new infantry regiment to be raised spe-cifically in Erie County. It was unknown how successful this recruiting effort would be, since three regiments had been raised in Erie County just the previous year. Yet in seven weeks of recruiting, more than 900 men made their way to Fort Porter in Buffalo to sign up. Training would come later.

"Large and very enthusiastic meetings are being held (war meetings) all over the country," reported Bennett, "a general war inspiration everywhere. James Ayer has con-sented to take command of a company of men ready to enlist if he will go out as captain. A large number of our finest young men enrolled."

Former town supervisor James Ayer, whose family had arrived in western New York from Massachusetts in 1811, was 49 years old when the president issued this call for volunteers. His elder brother Ira, also a former supervisor, was 60.[51]  Both volunteered for duty in the new 116th Infantry regiment, forming up that summer under the command of Col. Edward P. Chapin, a prominent Buffalo attorney returned to recuperate from a wound suffered in the fighting the previous May on the Peninsula.[52]

Ira Ayer, who had commanded a militia regiment during the Patriots' War scare of 1837, would be given command of Company A as captain.[53]  James, who was given a captaincy as well, would command Company K. Each company would have 80-100 officers and men. Both companies were raised principally from men in today's Southtowns, with Company K raised almost exclusively in the Town of Evans.

"August 10th," recalled Joseph,

a very solemn and interesting meeting at the Methodist Church in the evening. A Bible was presented to each member of the company [K], a number of clergymen present, each addressed the company.

On the . . . following day the boys left home for Fort Porter, there to await orders.

On September 3 the regiment was mustered in, and on September 5 nine of the ten companies of the 116th left Buffalo for Baltimore, where they would train for two

---

[51] Ira Ayer had been one of Joseph's companions on the 8-mile ox-sled ride in the winter of 1823-24.

[52] Chapin was also a member of Buffalo's first semi-pro baseball club, the Niagaras.

[53] Ira was obliged to resign his commission the following March, due to ill health and a general inability to withstand the rigors of army life in the field.

months.[54]  By December 13 they were at Ship Island, 20 miles off the coast of Mississippi, and after two weeks further drill, were landed on the Louisiana coast near New Orleans.

By this time McClellan had suffered immense losses at Antietam, and his replacement, Ambrose Burnside, had been decisively repulsed at Fredericksburg, also with great loss. The war in the Mississippi Valley, however, provided a glimmer of hope to the North. In December 1862 a determined and capable general named Grant began his lengthy and ultimately successful campaign against Vicksburg, on the Mississippi River. The Town of Evans men and the 116th, part of General Nathaniel P. Banks's army now, would participate—in cooperation with Grant's Vicksburg assault—in the following summer's siege of Port Hudson, Louisiana, 150 miles south of Vicksburg and just north of Baton Rouge.[55]  The surrender of Port Hudson a few days after the July 4 fall of Vicksburg shook off the last vestige of Confederate control over the Mississippi, prompting Lincoln's remark that "the Father of Waters again goes unvexed to the sea."

A high price was paid for the opening of the Mississippi. Among the heavy Union casualties at Port Hudson was Col. Chapin himself, who, while leading a charge against the Confederate works, received a ball through the head. The Evans men paid their share of the price. Among their casualties was James Ayer, who had proven unable to cope with the disease-ridden Louisiana swamps. He had fallen ill shortly after arrival there, and died at Baton Rouge on May 22.

---

[54] Company K was allowed a short furlough, entraining for Baltimore on September 10.

[55] The 48-day siege of Port Hudson, where Confederates were outnumbered by Union troops nearly 6 to 1, was the longest in American history. Both sides, but especially the Confederates, suffered grievously. The Confederate fortress was commanded by Maj. Gen. Franklin Gardner, a New Yorker.

# In the Shadow of War

♣

Following the departure of the 116th in September 1862, life proceeded uneasily, but proceed it did. "Business and time monotinous [sic]," noted Joseph, "days and weeks comeing [sic] and going, and with it life." In October Seymour's office at the Port of Buffalo was burglarized and $1,700 stolen from the safe. "No clew to the thief," remarked Joseph.

On January 1, 1863, Bennett not only took notice of the president's issuing of the Emancipation Proclamation that day, but also of an event of more personal importance: "On the first day of January, 1863, I handed over the books and papers to the newly appointed Clerk of the Board of Superintendents of Poor. My term of office expired yesterday. I stay in the Office a few days to instruct the new Superintendent and Clerk in the business of the office."

"I am now home again," he continued, "with my family, which is very satisfactory. Have been away almost constantly for the last 2 years."

The 59-year-old Evans farmer had completed the last public assignment of his life. Or so he thought.

In March 1863, the federal government, faced with declining enthusiasm for this bloody war, implemented a general draft. Only in areas where enlistment quotas were not being met would the draft actually go into effect, and very few men who served during the remainder of the war had actually been drafted, but its purpose was to "encourage" men to enlist. Provision was made for a man to hire a substitute, and many did. Until 1864, the draft could also be evaded by payment of $300. The draft was hugely unpopular. In anti-draft riots that would take place that summer in New York City, an estimated 500 people would be killed.

In late May, Joseph Bennett was appointed by the Provost Marshall of Buffalo as Enrolling Officer, "to enroll all persons liable to and for military duty." He reached his enrollment quota by the end of June. It is unclear whether his 28-year-old son Judson came under his jurisdiction; in any case, the young man—married a year and a half previous, and by now a father—was soon drafted.[56] Noted Judson's father, "A substitute was provided."

At this same time Bennett received the sad news of James Ayer's death. "He died of fever," commented Joseph, "a great loss to his family, to his Army company he commanded, to the church, and community. He was much more than ordinarily intelectual [sic] and inteligent [sic] and a devoted Christian man." Ayer's body would not be received in Evans for another nine months.

As June turned into July Bennett noted that "the uniformed militia of the state are called to Washington. The rebels are invading Pennsylvania." Then on July 7: "Good news from the Army in all directions, Vicksburgh surrendered on the 4th. Lee whipped in Pennsylvania."

By mid-August he had found enough leisure time to take a trip with Mary. On August 19 they boarded the luxury steamer *Fountain City* for the five-day lake journey to Chicago, then Amboy, to visit the Barrells. Following three weeks with Jane and Henry, they returned home by train, stopping to see Joseph's brother Alonzo and sister Sarah along the way.

On his return he noted with satisfaction that farm-product prices were excellent, that wool in particular was selling for 75 cents a pound.

On February 10, 1864, Ira Ayer arrived with the bodies of his brother James and three other Evans men, all for burial with military honors. Bennett served as Marshall for the occasion, terming it "a very solemn day." The mood was more upbeat the following week, when Evans men who had been serving on cavalry duty arrived

---

[56] Judson had married Nancy Taylor on November 7, 1861. Their son Fred was born September 9, 1862.

home on furlough and were thrown "a splendid supper and entertainment."

On May 29, another young person was taken, this time a person very dear to Joseph's heart: Seymour's young wife, Susan, who died of "black diphtheria" on this date in Buffalo.[57] "A good woman is gone," he lamented,

> What mysteries and troubles we have to contend with in life. A wife and young mother with health, and fair prospects for the future, to be so suddenly taken, seems *terrible*, is *crushing*. But our Heavenly Father knows best. We all attended the solemn funeral. My wife and Etta [Henrietta] stayed a day or two with Seymour. They brought home the little motherless child. Better she will stay with us.

In early August, probably to get his son's mind, as much as his own, off this shocking void in their life, 61-year old Joseph took Seymour fishing in the Thousand Islands. They and a friend booked passage on an over-night steamer from Lewiston to Clayton, near the head of the St. Lawrence, rented a boat and fished for three days. "Came home all right with a good lot of pickeral [sic]," pronounced Joseph. A "fine time."

"Am almost always at home," he commented now, "and time and business very monotinous [sic]. But enjoy my surroundings and family more than I can tell." Perhaps this feeling of well-being was enhanced by the presence of 6-year-old Belle in his home. "Am prospered in every way," he concluded. In September his world became even rosier when Jane and Henry arrived from Illinois. But he couldn't forget his departed young daughter-in-law. "All together except poor Susie," he said. "She is in heaven."

He expressed happiness that his sons Seymour and Judson, joint owners of a small boat engaged in lake hauling, were "running their vessel in the coal trade,"

---

[57] "Black" refers to the color of the leather-like membrane forming in the victim's nose, throat, or airway.

although in fact they were to sell the boat a few months later.

In January 1865 he noted the arrival of Thaddeus Seeley—his ward since childhood and now a physician and army veteran—from a mining venture in Arizona. The following month he noted the departure of his last two daughters from home: 34-year-old Etta to Ohio and 28-year-old Josephine to Illinois, both to teach.

His journal at this point becomes filled with quick jottings:

"Fine sleighing this winter."

"Little Belle . . . is with us and will stay, a fine little girl. We love her ever so much."

April 6: "A number of persons were injured badly, in telegraph office at Angola, by electric fluid from lightning."

On April 9, even though he reported hearing "good news from the army," the nature of the news must not have been clear because he said no more about it. Two days later, in fact, he noted, "Another draft of men for the army from the Town of Evans. A number were taken from this town."

But then it became clear that the terrible trial was actually ending: "News has just come to us that Genl. Lee surrendered his forces day before yesterday to Genl. Grant. The capitulation was signed in a farm house near Appomattox Court House. Lee's army had been terribly slaughtered. This was the death blow to the rebels." Fortunately he could not see into the future, or such jubilation would have been impossible. A new national sadness lay but a few days away.

"The 15th day of April," he wrote,

I left home very early in the morning in a buggy for Buffalo. On my way down, I left the main road, went over onto the Whites Corners Plank Road.[58]  When I

---

[58] The White's Corners Plank Road is present-day South Park Avenue, running from Main St. in today's Village of Hamburg northward to Buffalo. It was most easily accessed from the lake road via

came in sight of the toll gate, saw a number of men standing togather [sic]. As I drove up they appeared very sober, asked me if I had heard the news. What news? President Lincoln is dead, was assassinated last evening in a theater. I think I never experianced [sic] such feelings before. If been on my feet am sure I should have fallen.

I drove into Buffalo. Every person I saw, seemed in deep mourning, not a smile upon any countenance, the whole city dressed in mourning. Never saw such a sight, and never expect to again. Black cloth hung in festoons from window to window. Where so much black cloth came from I cannot imagine. Party feeling seemed to be lost sight of, all mourned alike. Only heard of one exulting case. A man went into a saloon and said to the proprietor, What do you think of your little god now? Proprietor came slowly arround [sic] his counter, kicked the man out onto the sidewalk, and from the sidewalk into the gutter. I think if he had killed the man, a jury could not be found that would convict him.

Not a man would talk business. Came home without accomplishing anything. *Glad of it.* All mourn, the people mourn, the nation mourns.

Glad the feeling was such that no business could be done.

Four days later he attended a memorial service "at the same hour in which the funeral of President Lincoln was held at the Presidential Mansion in Washington."

"Also in all the churches in the Northern states," he continued. "What a funeral, what mourning."

Trying to return to some degree of normalcy by focusing on simple things, he reported in May that he was "at-

---

Big Tree Road, which joins it near today's Southwestern Boulevard (US 20). It is likely that Joseph took this route from the lake.
There were three toll gates on the plank road between Hamburg and Buffalo.

tending to [his] domestic and farm duties," and that he had even sold ten cows at $45 each.

But now, as if the tumultuous events of the past year had not been enough, on July 15 he received a further blow in the news that his 54-year-old brother Samuel had died.[59]

"Died of heart disease," he declared. "Another of our numerous family gone. He was a Christian man of more than ordinary inteligence [*sic*]. I expect a son of his will come and live with us."

Nearly 62 years old, Joseph Bennett would permit his house gradually to fill up with children, and later, strangers, doubtless hoping they might assuage his growing sadness.

---

[59] Samuel had lived in Belvidere, Illinois, for many years but now lived in Monticello, Minnesota, where he passed away. His wife Celestia had predeceased him by several years, and he had remarried. He and Celestia had had at least two sons, one named Jason. Samuel had served one term in the Minnesota state senate, and had held various other political offices.

WASHINGTON STREET BAPTIST CHURCH, NORTHEAST
CORNER OF WASHINGTON AND SWAN, BUFFALO, NEW YORK
– Joseph Bennett gathered many of the building materials, chiefly
brick, for the construction of this church in 1835-36. The building was
razed in 1900. The structure in the background is the First Universalist Church. Photo taken prior to 1866, when the First Universalist
Church was razed.

*Courtesy Town of Evans Historical Society*

JOSEPH BENNETT – This photo may have been taken as early as Bennett's term in the New York State assembly, or as late as his tenure on the Erie County Poor Board. He appears to be in his fifties.

*Source: National Archives and Records Service*

AFTERMATH OF BATTLE, PORT HUDSON, LOUISIANA, 1863 – Western New York's 116th Infantry regiment participated in this lengthy siege, costly in American lives. Col. Edward Chapin, a prominent Buffalo attorney, was killed here leading a charge against the Confederate works. Companies A and K of the 116th were made up chiefly of Southtowns men.

*Courtesy David Ritchie Carr*

SEYMOUR BENNETT, ABOUT 1875 – Born in 1828, Seymour was Joseph and Mary Bennett's eldest child. Following in his father's footsteps as a provider of hospitality services, he turned 15 wooded lakeside acres of his father's original farmland into Bennett Park, building a hotel, cabins, and tenting and dining facilities there. Seymour, who had one child, outlived his father by only 11 years, passing away in 1910.

JOSEPHINE BENNETT, ABOUT 1870 – Josephine, born in 1837, was the youngest of the Bennetts' five children. In 1866 she married her parents' former ward, Dr. Thaddeus P. Seeley. The couple had three children, two of whom died young. Both Josephine and Thaddeus would predecease Joseph, the former dying in 1896, and the latter in 1898.

*Courtesy David Ritchie Carr*

SUSAN ISABELLA, OR BELLE, BENNETT, ABOUT 1885 – Belle was born in 1858 to Seymour Bennett and Susan Barton. She was Seymour's only child. In 1889 she married Henry O'Hara of Toronto, and moved there with him. The couple would have three children. As a child, following her mother's death, Belle had lived with Joseph and Mary Bennett. As an adult, prior to her marriage, she would help her grandfather Joseph and her widowed Aunt Jane with the boarding and camping business.

*Courtesy David Ritchie Carr*

*Courtesy David Ritchie Carr*

JOSEPH BENNETT WITH GREAT-GRANDCHILDREN, MAY 1899, FIVE MONTHS BEFORE HIS DEATH – Pictured with Joseph at the Bennett homestead in Evans are, from left to right, Seymour, baby Marion, and Lilian O'Hara, the three children of Belle and Henry O'Hara, of Toronto. Henry took the picture.

# 7

# *ENDINGS AND BEGINNINGS*

During the period following the Civil War, it becomes more difficult to sort Joseph Bennett's days into definable groupings. He had more than three decades to live, and he would spend this period following the same continuum of physical and mental activity and service to others that had characterized his life until now. His health appears to have held up as he approached his mature years, and he took life as it came. As is normal with the aged, though, death flitted more frequently into his peripheral vision. Disease and death stalked his own generation most aggressively, but they appear to have stalked the young with almost equal zeal. He encountered them frequently within his community, and, disconcertingly often during these years, within his family.

On August 21, 1865, he wrote, "Old Mr. Barton [the father of Susan, his son Seymour's recently deceased wife] came up from Buffalo and informed us that Seymour was quite sick. My wife went immediately down and brought Seymour home." He continued, "Dr. T.P. Seeley came a day or two since, and will attend Seymour." The Bennetts' eldest son, 36 years old at the time, was diagnosed with typhoid fever. With the faith in the medical profession common in those grasping for hope, he added, "I think it very fortunate for Seymour that Dr. Seeley is here." To help ensure Seymour's recov-

# Joseph Bennett

ery, George Sweetland, the town's iconic physician, was called in consultation. By September 11 the patient was reported as improving, with Joseph giving all credit to the medical men, particularly Seeley.

Young Dr. Seeley stayed with the Bennetts until October 20, when he decided that his patient was out of danger, and went home.

By November, the 62-year-old Joseph had been sought out for public service yet again. "Appointed Commissioner of Highways," he noted, "and accepted reluctantly." It is unclear if this was a county or town position, but in either case it was guaranteed to take him away from what he loved. "I am attending to my family and farm business," he wrote. "Find it much more pleasant than public business. I do so love a domestic life. Feel independent and happy." Church life was also important to him. "Very much enjoy Church privileges," he remarked, "and society of kindred spirits."

Susan's father, Phineas Barton, Jr., no doubt drawn by the presence of his granddaughter Belle in the Bennett household, started to make frequent visits at this time. The Bennetts also began to see Susan's sister more often. She had married a man named Ferris.

On November 16 the Bennett home was augmented by another young person. "Jason Bennett," noted Joseph, "my brother Samuel's son, 13 years of age, came . . . to live with us. Poor boy has neither father or mother. We take him and calculate care for him as our own." It is unclear why Jason did not remain with Samuel's second wife.

We as readers of Joseph Bennett's journal may not see it coming, but the Bennetts surely did. On February 1, 1866, their youngest daughter Josephine and their former ward, Dr. Thaddeus Seeley, were married. Thad's brother John, also a former ward of the Bennetts, came to the wedding from Potsdam with his wife. The Bartons, father and daughter, came, as did some Sweetlands, some Cashes, Judge Salisbury's widow Ann, and others. "The excitement now over," wrote the bride's father fol-

# Endings and Beginnings

lowing the festivities. "We sit down and try to imagine the result of our daughter's marriage. We have confidence in her companion, and confidently trust that God blesses the union."

Sixteen days later Phineas Barton was dead of a heart attack. Bennett was stunned. "Good man gone, only three weeks or less was at the wedding of our daughter in apparently good health." He and Mary took little Belle to the funeral in Buffalo.

♧

Bennett's connections at this time paid off for his son Judson. In April he reported that Judson—like his brother Seymour before him—had been appointed Inspector of Customs at the Port of Buffalo. At this point in his life, his two sons lived and worked in Buffalo, and two of his three daughters—Jane and "Phene" (Josephine) had moved to Illinois. Etta had apparently returned from Ohio by this time. Yet he seems to have continued seeking out young people to replace his lost children. On June 4 he noted, "Went to Buffalo, obtained papers of guardianship for Caroline Hawks."

"I am at home, engaged in farming as usual," he continued. "My sons both away. The Sunday school occupies part of my time. Have been Superintendent of S. School between 30 and 40 years. Might be in much worse business."

Judson, he noted, was away from home most of the time. (He was frequently on the lake pursuing smugglers.)

John Seeley, brother of Thaddeus, and also Bennett's former ward, had married a Canadian woman named Curry.[60] Bennett's son Seymour, a widower now for two years, had conceived an interest in the new Mrs. Seeley's sister, had begun to court her, and on August 14, 1866, the two were married. "Seymour brot [sic] home his new

---

[60] There is some evidence that her surname was Coryell, not Curry.

wife," noted Joseph on August 17, "Lillie Curry, fine looking girl, *Canadian girl* . . . Time will tell the rest."

Oddly, little Belle, Seymour's daughter, continued to live with her grandparents—not with her father and stepmother.

On September 26, Bennett notes an unpleasant occurrence. He and Mary were entertaining a Customs officer—possibly Judson's boss—and Judson himself. Judson and "Mr. Myster" had arrived from Buffalo by horse and buggy, and had put up the horse in Bennett's barn while they dined, intending to leave immediately after dinner, doubtless in order to reach Buffalo before dark. Following dinner, wrote Bennett, "they went to the carriage house not more than four rods from the house. Horse gone, can never get any trace or track of the horse—*adroitly done.*"

♣

By early December the area's usual lake-effect snows had arrived. "Snow in December 2-1/2 feet deep," recorded Joseph, "and increased to 3 feet. Trains were stopped for some days. At least five locomotives, in one train, worked through." Then on January 1: "Snow continues very deep. Cars have been blocked again for the last few days. No such depth of snow or stormy month since 1830 or 1831, have forgotten which." The snows continued. On February 7 he wrote, "The past month has been another severe month, snow from 2 to 3 feet all through the month."

February brought no relief from precipitation, except that it had begun to liquefy. "March 1st," wrote Bennett, "have passed through another severe month of cold, snow, rain, high water." Living at the edge of ice-jammed Big Sister Creek, his property doubtless experienced flooding.

The 63-year old Bennett had for some time been considering how to keep his farm productive in the face of his advancing years, and in the spring of 1867 brought

# Endings and Beginnings

in a farmer named Emil Bock, with his family, to live on the property and to work the farm on shares.

His summer appeared to go well. The farm was under control and he and Mary had time for relaxation and family visits. "Myself and the boys," he noted, "are keeping a fine sail boat for pleasure and enjoy it ever so much. Am still engaged Sabbath school work and enjoy that. My nephew, Jason, is still with us." Sometime in May or June his sister, 57-year-old Sarah, and his 46-year-old brother Valentine arrived from Michigan, the latter with his wife Marcia and only surviving child, Achsah Adelaide, about 12.[61] Valentine, a country doctor who had lived in California and Michigan, was transporting his family in early summer 1867 to their new home in Newfield, New Jersey. After a few days in Evans they moved on, but Sarah remained for a time. On June 24 the Bennetts played host to another of Mary Roat Bennett's sisters, Margaret, who had married a Joseph Richards and had spent the recent war in Nashville. "They are splendid people," remarked Bennett. "But," he continued in a more critical aside, "were rebels during the war and are tinctured yet."

On November 8 he notes the passage through Evans of "the Great Pedestrian Weston." Edward Payson Weston, in a foretaste of today's Guinness Book enthusiasm, had set himself the goal of walking from Portland, Maine, to Chicago within 30 consecutive days—a period running from noon of October 29 to noon of November 28. The distance had been calculated at 1,234 miles, which might have meant walking about 40 miles a day, except for Weston's bow to the mores of his time: he would not, he announced, walk during the 24 hours of any of the four Sabbaths falling during this period. Due probably to the fact—reported by Bennett—that, early in his trip, he covered 100 miles in a single day, he also required a fifth day off for recovery, leaving him only 25 days to accomplish his feat.

---

[61] Valentine's other children had died in infancy.

# Joseph Bennett

Weston limped into Chicago on November 28, one hour and twenty minutes before noon.

The year 1867 wound down slowly for Bennett. "Farming season over, pretty good season," he noted at the end of November. "My daughter Josephine left for Chicago, expecting to be gone some months." He commented on the death of Whiting Cash, "one of the oldest residents in western New York," and, on December 10, of his "settling the estate of Carrie Hawks, with the estate of L.H. Hawks, and getting her portion into government bonds."

When he made this entry, neither he nor his neighbors could know that in one week their town would be the scene of a widely reported disaster.

In railroad parlance, a "frog" is the crossing of two rails, where a device causes the wheels of a railroad train to move smoothly from one track to another.

In 1867, as eastbound trains approached the 160-foot long railroad bridge over Big Sister Creek, located about 2,000 feet east of Angola Station, they were routinely moved from one track to another by a frog placed a few hundred feet west of the bridge. On December 18, the engineer of an eastbound express composed of four baggage and mail cars and four passenger coaches was trying to make up a nearly three-hour delay in his run from Cleveland to Buffalo and points east. The trainmen were getting all they could out of their machine as it roared through Angola without stopping and headed for the bridge that spanned the 40-foot-deep Big Sister ravine.

Unknown to the crew, the forward axle in the rear truck of the rear car, a passenger coach, was slightly bent, causing a small wobble in a wheel. Under normal circumstances this was a non-problem, but, in the circumstances that were rapidly approaching, it would become a serious one. When the affected wheel struck the frog, the rear truck jumped the track, instantly derailing

150

the last car. With the equipment then in use, the train could not have been stopped between the frog and the bridge, even if the accident had been noted by the engine crew. The car was therefore dragged onto the bridge, bumping over ties, swaying violently, and soon pulling the car in front of it off the tracks. As the head of the train passed the far end of the bridge, the rear car slid off the track and slipped tail-first into the creek, coming to rest vertically against the far abutment. The remaining crippled car held onto the track, but broke loose on the other side of the bridge and rolled down the embankment. In this car only one passenger was killed.

The passengers in the rear coach—44 in number—were less fortunate. The car had been heated by two iron woodstoves, one at each end. As the coach slammed vertically against the bridge abutment, the heavy "uphill" stove fell—sparks and embers flying—on top of the trapped passengers, in the process igniting the car's plush interior. Accounts vary, but as many as 41 passengers in this car may have perished, most of the bodies being badly burned. Passengers in both cars were seriously injured.

"The excitement tremendous," wrote Bennett in the aftermath of this event, which caused a brief sensation nationally as the Great Angola Train Disaster. "People from all parts of the country looking for friends dead or alive. My daughter Etta was very active in watching and nursing."

One of the first to arrive at the scene was Angola's Dr. Curtis. It is likely that Etta was doing her "watching and nursing" alongside the doctor, because it was he to whom she would be married four months later.

♣

In February Bennett reported that the mercury had dipped to 25 below zero on the 3rd of the month, but that sleighing was fine. Time, however, remained heavy on his hands. "Weeks and months pass monotinous [sic]," he noted, "the greatest change, wrinkles in the face."

# Joseph Bennett

On April 22 he recorded the marriage of Henrietta, his only remaining unmarried daughter, to Dr. Curtis. It was a small wedding. "Wedding guests select," he said. "Relatives only from Evans and Buffalo. Another child will leave the parental roof. God only knows the result."

It was fortunate for the Bennetts that God was the only one to know the result, for an approaching tragedy would considerably exceed their worst fears.

"Dr. Curtis and Etta gone to keeping house in Angola," he wrote. "Dr. Curtis stands very high in his profession."

In June he and son Seymour journeyed to Chicago to attend the Republican National Convention, at which U.S. Grant was nominated as the party's candidate in the coming presidential election. Joseph was well pleased by the outcome. "A very harmonious convention," he declared, "and a good ticket." While there, the two conventioneers took the opportunity of visiting with Josephine and Thaddeus Seeley.

"Terribly warm," he remarked, "during the month of June, ranges at about 90 for days." But he escaped the heat by moving onto the water. "We have a very fine sail boat," he noted, "a delight to the boys, *pleases me pretty well too*. Judson spend [sic] much time on the lake after smugglers. The same monotinous [sic] farmers life continues."

But by the beginning of August his mind was no longer on heat or sailboats or the monotony of a farmer's existence, for his newlywed daughter Etta had fallen alarmingly ill. "Trouble of the heart and fever" was his layman's appreciation of her illness. She sank quickly. Other doctors were called in, but to no avail. "She died on the 6th of August," he wrote, "in her mother's arms. She had been married only three and a half months. God knows why. To us terrible. Dr. Curtis seems almost crazy, he rebels *but must submit*."

Henrietta Bennett Curtis, sadly predeceasing her parents at the age of 35, was buried on her father's 65th

# Endings and Beginnings

birthday, August 8, 1868, at the Forest Avenue cemetery in Angola.

♣

As the eventful summer wound itself down, and green leaves began to metamorphose into fiery reds and brilliant yellows, a likely already-morose Joseph glumly reported that on October 5, Monroe Aldrich, a neighbor, had committed suicide by cutting his throat with a razor. "Found dead in his orchard," he commented.

In one of those odd juxtapositions of thought that occur to us all, however, he went on not about suicide but about the product of orchards: "We sent a lot of fruit to our children, in Chicago and Amboy. Fruit from home seems better than from any other place."

Josephine had been pregnant for some months now, and in December, as Josephine's time approached, Mary Bennett journeyed to Illinois. On December 22 Josephine gave birth to a boy whom she named Alfred.

The summer of 1869, with the scars of war still tender throughout the nation and a still unreconstructed South seething from its recent defeat, Joseph passed off with a laconic, "Summer gone with no particular change." He does report baptisms in the church and his continuing passion—shared by his two sons—for sailing.

In late October the 66-year-old Joseph and 60-year-old Mary embarked upon a trip to revisit the scenes of their youth, 40 years previous. On the 25th of October," he wrote,

> left Evans for Buffalo, then took N.Y. and Erie Road, and arrived in Harrisburgh next morning. From there took cars up the Susquehanna River, to the head of the Pennsylvania Canal, on the east side of the river. Curiosity led me once more to see the heavy canal work that I had charge in building 42 years since, and have not seen for that last number of years.

# Joseph Bennett

He found the work he had done four decades earlier "standing first rate," but was shocked to find only two persons alive that he knew from those days.

If people had departed, however, the places—to the Bennetts' joy—had remained constant. "I went to the house and room in which my wife and I were married. The house, the room, and surroundings just the same, entirely unchanged. Forty-two years since."

Strangely, Bennett seems, over the years, to have lost track of his Uncle Seymour, who had been one of his favorite relatives, and whom he spent some time now in seeking out. He could find no trace of this once-close uncle, only ten years his senior, and for whom his first child had been named.

"At last found a lady that knew all about my uncle and family," he wrote. "My uncle and wife had died some years since and that a daughter was living in the city and married to Mr. Taylor."[62]

"I went to see the daughter," he continued, "Mrs. Mariah Taylor . . . Where ever I go, I find that death has made its ravages. Wherever I go, I find time hath made its mark."

Unable to find himself so close to the field on which was fought the largest battle ever in the western hemisphere and not go to see it, he wasted no time in boarding a train for Gettysburg, where he arrived on October 27. Sharing a carriage rental with an Ohio man, he went over the ground with this companion and a guide, visiting as well the monument to the Union fallen. "One of the most interesting days of my life," was his comment.

He and Mary then took the train to Baltimore, New York, and home.

As Bennett aged, his journal entries grew both sparse and spare. Following his notation after his Gettysburg

---

[62] Seymour's wife, Maria McKinley Bennett, had died in 1851, and Seymour in 1853. Both are buried in Harrisburg.

# Endings and Beginnings

trip that time was "rolling on very monotinous [*sic*]," with its "usual casualties," he made no substantial entries until the end of September 1870, when he recorded a railroad trip that he, Mary, and Josephine took to Potsdam to visit John Seeley and family. "Found John Seeley and family in health," he noted, "and good condition finantially [*sic*]." From Potsdam the trio moved on to Ogdensburg, and from Ogdensburg—via steamer and the Welland Canal—to Port Colborne. Josephine continued by steamer to Chicago, and her parents returned to Buffalo by train.

"In due time," noted Joseph, "all arrived at our several homes all right."

In November, Republican Bennett received an Election Day shock. "November election," he wrote, "all gone *Democratic* in county and state. Queer, isn't it?"

November also heralded the arrival of a familiar visitor, but one normally making a December entry. "Severe snow storm from Nov. 21st," he said, "continued until 27. Snow 3 feet deep and very tedious." He had to face more than snow, however, at this time nearly losing his very home. "In one night during the storm," he wrote, "our house took fire in the cellar way. My nephew Jason was awakened by the dense smoke in his room and gave the alarm. If he had slept five minutes longer all would have been lost, and we turned out in a terrible storm houseless and naked. Providence interposed."

"We suppose," he concluded, "the servant girl left a burning candle in the candle box, or stair way."

At an age when many of his worn-out contemporaries were either eyeing a rocking chair or deceased, the 67-year-old Bennett still relished and pursued the outdoor life that he had always loved. "In the month of February (about the 28th)," he wrote, "fitted out an ice boat on the lake. She works well."

At the height of summer that year (1871), he wrote that his "boys" were "enthusiastic over sail boats." He then quietly confided that, despite having had to miss

155

church "for a long time" due to an ear and throat ailment, he was "somewhat in the spirit" of sailing himself.

Death, of course, continued to lurk at the edges of his life, dashing in at times to make an unexpected claim. Young Jason received a letter from his brother that his 15-year-old stepsister had just died in Minneapolis. Joseph's brother-in-law, Elder Jacob Price (Sarah's husband) passed away on August 7 in Cassopolis. Michigan. "A highly educated divine and greatly respected," commented Joseph. "He leaves a large and devoted family to mourn him, also the Church and community."

On August 23 he and Seymour took their sailboat on a three-day trip to the Grand River, Ontario, across the lake from Dunkirk, and two weeks later he left for Chicago, as before, aboard the steamer *Fountain City*. He found Mary, who had left before him, at the Seeleys, ready for the arrival of a new baby, who turned out to be a little girl, to be named Mamie.

Leaving Chicago for home on September 22, he and Mary missed by 16 days the famous incineration of the city attributed to Mrs. O'Leary's cow. The Chicago fire was, at that time, the greatest fire in American history. "I am sorry," he wrote, somewhat wistfully, on October 9, "we did not stay a few days longer in Chicago that we might witness the fire. Every one reads the history of the great Chicago fire." It does not appear that the Seeleys were affected by the fire.

On May 13, 1872, he noted that there was still ice in the lake's eastern basin. "Lots of ice," he wrote, "in the bay above Buffalo. For the last few days vessels have been gathering in above the ice, about 50 waiting to get through the ice into the harbor."

The election of 1872, in which President Grant was reelected, pleased him much more than had the election of 1870. "The election this fall is *glorious*," he declared. "Republicans carry every Northern state."

In April 1873, after noting a visit from his 55-year-old sister Lucina Gibson, whom he had not seen since 1856, he remarked that he had another sister as well as a

# Endings and Beginnings

brother (49-year-old Caroline and 58-year-old Thomas) whom he had not seen in 38 years, when they moved west with their parents. "How I would like a family reunion," he exclaimed.

Around this time Jane's husband Henry Barrell, who appears to have been staying with Joseph and Mary, was taken ill and began to fail quickly. The diagnosis was consumption. Henry's illness, however, receded briefly into the background on receipt of even more tragic news: on January 12, 1874, the Bennetts learned of the death of Josephine and Thad Seeley's 2-1/2-year-old daughter Mamie, cause unknown to us. "Really," he wrote, "a beautiful child."

In March 1874 Joseph recorded that Henry Barrell's parents had come from Illinois to visit their son. They returned home, he said, "never expecting to see [him] again. A very affecting scene when they parted with Henry." Henry held on throughout the spring, but was clearly failing.

In April, during Henry's illness, Bennett noted an event that would become a cause célèbre in Evans: O.H. Dibble's troubled son, Orange, or O.J., assaulted his wife (Betsy Sweetland, daughter of Dr. George Sweetland) with an axe, "evidently," as Bennett wrote, "intending to kill her."

"She fought and saved herself," he continued, "whiskey the cause." O.J. Dibble was eventually adjudged insane, but it would take three years and another attempted murder (this time of his wife's brother George) to get him committed to an institution.

On July 23, 1874, Henry Barrell died. "A good young man has gone," wrote Bennett. My daugh. Jane is left, a sad, *heart broken* widow."

Evidently referring to the eventual deaths of those left behind, he continued, "Only a little while, a little while, and a reunion."

"Henry died a Christian," continued Joseph, "was highly respected by all who knew him. He left behind him a good and honorable record."

157

# Joseph Bennett

Jane spent a few days in Buffalo with friends before returning to her parents in Evans. In September she headed back to Illinois, moving in with the Seeleys.

In June 1875 it appears that Bennett was asked by a family named Walker, who had noticed the idyllic setting in which the Bennetts lived, if the family could pitch tents on their land and stay awhile. Joseph said yes. Two months later a Mrs. Marsh, her sister, and a sick child—probably looking for healthy country air—asked if the Bennetts might consider taking on a few boarders for the remainder of the summer. Joseph said yes. Other families arrived, pitching tents and joining the Bennetts at table. Apparently so many came that a doctor was called in to oversee the sanitary aspects of camping and boarding.

Joseph said yes to it all and the final chapter of his life was opened.

# 8

# MILES TO GO

By September 1876 Joseph Bennett had completed 73 years, but the rocking chair would have to wait for a while. This year marked the nation's centenary, and the Evans patriot, who had seen such monumental change in his town and county, and whose life reached back almost to the nation's founding, saw no better way to participate than to journey to Philadelphia to the great Centennial Exhibition. He went with David Barrell of Fredonia, his daughter Jane, and others. Mary remained in New York to visit relatives.

Of the Exhibition he remarked, "Most wonderful, great and grand display." He commented on the acreage of every building on the grounds—the main building alone, he said, covered 21-1/2 acres—and he reported the value of all buildings together at $8.5 million.

Despite his interest in the world outside his town, he seemed increasingly to miss the stimulation common in his earlier life, but nonetheless noted that "health, and the comforts of life, and means of doing some good" continued to him.

♧

"It is now April 1877," he wrote. "Another winter has passed, with only ordinary change, except that we have been repairing the house."

# Joseph Bennett

He reported further campers on his land, commenting that his guests "enjoy it hugely."

"Our people," he said, indicating that he was perhaps not intimately involved with the guest operation himself, "are having a large number of boarders this summer."

A year later, in March, he noted "another winter gone and no great visible changes with us." Then: "Wife is not very well and has not been for some months, but is around as usual."

Much to Bennett's surprise, a piece of his former life, missing for years, was at this time reinstated. "At the annual Town Meeting," he announced, "I am elected supervisor for the coming year." He was 74 years old. He soon began attending sessions of the Board of Supervisors in Buffalo, likely pleased to be back in the traces. At home, the number of campers and boarders was increasing, but he left all in the hands of his widowed daughter Jane.

As 1878 blended into 1879, following a few customary observations about the winter ("Snow in December 28 inches deep . . . Sleighing splendid during the month of January, everyone seems to enjoy it.") came the darkest paragraphs of his journal. At noon on February 3, 1879, Mary, his wife of 51 years, suddenly died. "This is the sadest [sic] day of my life," he confided to his diary,

> My dear little wife . . . how *terrible* how *crushing*. This forenoon was as well as she had been for months, was out in the snow, turning a large piece of cloth she was bleaching. She died suddenly without any warning, until she was nearly gone, entirely unexpected to me. The bereavement seems rather greater than I am able to bear. We have lived . . . *very happy*. What a *loss*, *what a loss* to me, the family, and the Church. I know I must submit but cannot feel reconciled. We have this consolation, that all who knew her, loved her. I know I am not the only one bereaved. All the family mourn, and mourn deeply. Oh, another sad day, the funeral, day after tomorrow.

# Miles to Go

Mary's funeral was from the Bennett home on February 5. She was laid to rest in the family plot in Angola. The Bennett children, having thought only that she was a little ill, were devastated. "Our children . . .," continued Joseph, "are sadly mourning the loss of a mother, and all strive to comfort me."

"Time rolls heavily on," he said finally.

As all know who have lost a loved one, no matter the difficulty, life must go on for those left behind. In Bennett's case this meant preparing for campers and boarders, and he began to throw himself more fully into the business. He noted that they were keeping thirty boarders that summer, using a long tent for a dining room. Fourteen campers had arrived via railroad from St. Louis. Missouri. "Angola," observed the *Angola Record* of July 24, "is becoming noted as a summer resort and is one of the most pleasant places at which to spend a short vacation."

Bennett began to think of expanding the operation by bringing his own home more fully into service. "I am raising the house one story higher," he wrote, "which will enlarge the house very much." Jane continued to superintend the business, and generally to manage all household affairs for him.

The house was occupied not only by guests, but also by one John Clark, who had been invited by Joseph to work the farm on shares for the following year. Clark would soon rent the farm, and Joseph would be out of the farming business for the first time in more than half a century. Joseph was doing his best to keep his mind occupied, but he found it difficult. "The summer and fall," he wrote, "have gone very . . . sad, to me."

In January 1880, his habitual concern for the less fortunate backfired on him. "We took a boy from the orphan asylum," he noted, "by the name of George Perkins, who proved to be a fraud. He had an excellent mother in

# Joseph Bennett

Brantford, Canada, from whome [*sic*] he had runn [*sic*] away."

On March 19, 1880, he recorded that they had just finished putting ice into the icehouse, "the thickest only 3 inches thick."

"It has been an unusually warm winter," he continued, "no ice in the lake now, or has been during the winter."

The following summer he noted the presence of boarders again, and that he was "enlarging every summer." Among the guests were families from Rochester and Cleveland. By fall he was putting the finishing touches on a new dining hall, but he took time off in late October for a Republican rally in Buffalo, attended by former president Grant himself.

The *Angola Record* that summer, among notices of extraordinary sturgeon catches in Dibble's Bay (100 in one day, one specimen weighing in at 130 lb.) and the novel appearance of bicycles in the town (two cyclists had ridden out from Buffalo in two hours), gave the following description of the Bennett family's burgeoning resort facilities:

> There are few places of summer resort in the vicinity of Buffalo that present such combined attractions, and which have become so popular with our society people, as the camping grounds near Angola. About three miles from the station is the Deacon Bennett farm, or "Lake Forest," adjoining which is the residence of his son, Judson Bennett.[63] Both farms are admirably situated on high land, and in a most beautiful and healthful spot, and have altogether about thirty commodious tents, which are perfectly waterproof and as comfortable as a home, even during wet weather. Deacon Bennett's farm is one of the most popular resorts in the vicinity and is a place where

---

[63] Lake Forest may take its name from the higher, wooded portion of Bennett's property eventually converted by Seymour Bennett into a resort called Bennett Park.

only people who are properly introduced may procure board. Judson Bennett's residence and camping ground, immediately adjoining, is called the Bluffs, is also select, and we guests here are also provided with every convenience and excellent fare.[64]

Two trains per day arrived in Angola. Passengers for the Bennetts were met at the station and taken by wagon to Joseph's or Judson's facilities.

Other camping facilities had appeared in response to a growing demand. City dwellers were coming to realize that they needn't spend their summers amid hot and steamy streets—that cool lake breezes lay but a short trainride away. The *Record* continued:

About two miles south, on the main road, is Cash's camp, which also has a good share of the visitors. For about two miles in a tortuous manner, the "Gonagegee Creek", or as the Indians called it, the black water, wends its way to the lake, which at some seasons of the year, may be reached directly from the creek, but at present is closed by a narrow sand bar. On the beach there are bathing houses for ladies and gentlemen, which are daily used by both sexes, old and young; many of them have beautiful bathing costumes.[65]

The following summer the *Record* noted a baseball game set up between the young men staying at Joseph Bennett's camp and those staying at Judson's. A recent

---

[64] *Angola Record*, August 5, 1880. Sometime prior to 1880, Joseph had transferred to Judson the 50 acres of his property closest to the mouth of Big Sister Creek, upon which property Judson had built his home. Judson, possibly following his father's lead, had also established a camping facility there, calling it The Bluffs, later adding a resort hotel called Pine Lodge. Like his father's resort, Judson's facility became a popular destination for summer vacationers.

[65] Ibid.

# Joseph Bennett

concert at Joseph's camp was pronounced "far in advance of most amateur entertainments."[66]

September 1881 was marked by the death of president James Garfield, who had been shot by a disgruntled office-seeker as he boarded a train in Washington the previous July. "A terrible calamity, and great loss to the nation," commented Joseph.

During the fall of 1881 the first iron bridge was built across Big Sister Creek at the Bennett homestead, as the property was coming to be known. But the season was made even more memorable for Bennett by Josephine's arrival from Chicago with her 12-year-old son Alfred and his 6-year-old brother Bertie, who, like his deceased sister Mamie, was a sickly child. Alfred himself, or "Allie," as he was called, suffered from epilepsy.

In July 1882 Bennett noted the death of his sister-in-law Jane, wife of his long-time friend and mentor, O.H. Dibble. Dibble himself, having gone with his son Alfred to California in 1853 to prospect for gold, had died there in 1867. Young Alfred Dibble had married and stayed in California. At the end of the following month, John Clark, operator of Bennett's farm for the past four years, also died. And during the first week of September, the town's pioneer physician, Dr. George Sweetland, died. He had served since 1821, the very year that Evans had been carved from Eden, and Erie County from Niagara County. "No man ever lived in the Town of Evans missed like him," wrote Bennett.

> He has been in constant practice for sixty-one years, his fame was far and wide. Just as faithful to the poor where he never expected a cent, as to the rich.
>
> God has given him a long and useful life.

As he approached his 80th birthday, in the spring of 1883, Joseph noted that he and Jane were getting ready for another summer of boarders, and that they had built an addition to the dining room. According to the *Angola*

---

[66] *Angola Record*, July 28, 1881.

*Record*, Judson was also building. He had just finished constructing his two-story resort hotel—to be known as Pine Lodge—with dining space for 150 on the first floor and eight bedrooms on the second. The *Record* noted the presence of "quite a number of people at this place already."[67]

In late May, Joseph reported an event quite unrelated to facilities enlargement. "On May 25," he wrote, "Fred Bennett's boat was stolen by two men." Fred was his 20-year-old grandson (Judson's son), a law student. His grandfather seemed ambivalent about Fred's potential for success in life. The young man apparently had an adventurous turn of mind, and was perhaps a little unbalanced: 15 years hence, despite a promising legal career, he would abandon his family and disappear, never to be seen again in western New York.

On this date in 1883, once the alarm had been raised over the missing sailboat (spotted now heading out into the lake), Fred and the Bennetts' hired man threw a rifle into a rowboat and started to pull in pursuit. Since the thieves were judged to have a three-mile head start, the outcome for young Bennett was not promising. What kept him and his companion going was the fact that the thieves appeared to know little about sailing, and the oarsmen, rifle at the ready, steadily closed the gap. The thieves, also armed, threw some shots toward the pursuers, and Bennett returned fire.

At the end of a long day of pursuit, the sailboat grounded on the Canadian beach near the Grand River, 25 miles across the lake, with the doubtless exhausted pursuers now close behind. The thieves quickly vanished, but Bennett and his companion, on landing near the boat, saw that one or more of their shots had hit home, since the abandoned sailboat was bloodstained. The boat was recovered and brought home. No fallout from the shooting is mentioned.

---

[67] *Angola Record*, July 5, 1883.

# Joseph Bennett

♧

Josephine and Thaddeus Seeley had lost one child, and appeared to be on their way to losing another. Their boy Bertie seemed not to thrive. He was sent in the fall of 1883 to stay with his grandfather, who was uncomfortable with the responsibility. "Bertie is very nervous," wrote Joseph, "and not well at all." Anxious to return him to his father's care, he sent the 6-year-old back to Chicago—in the care of neighbors—in mid-February 1884.

The following June, at the age of 80, he attended his second Republican National Convention, this one in Chicago as well. "Chicago grows like a mushroom," he observed, "just wonderful."

On August 8 he celebrated his 81st birthday, receiving a number of gifts from his boarders—a napkin ring, a silk handkerchief, gold spectacles among them. At the conclusion of this season he asked rhetorically whether they would have another season. "I rather enjoy the excitement myself," he declared, "but Jane, poor girl, it is so hard for her."

In October, octogenarian Bennett embarked on yet another lengthy trip, this time with son Judson. "Took cars for Toronto," he wrote,

> there took steamer down Lake Ontario during the afternoon and night. In the morning, the steamer entered the [St. Lawrence] River at Kingston, and down among the Thousand Islands, and through the various rapids during the day. At night too dark to run farther, the steamer came to along side a dock about fifteen or twenty miles above Montreal. In the morning the famous Indian Pilot, Baptiste, came on board and run the steamer through the noted Lachine rapids. Truly a very exciting run. Arrived in Montreal, took in the city during the day. It is an old and seems a prosperous city. Streets generally irregular, narrow and at present, filthy. Has the appearance of a large maratime [sic] business. In the evening we left Mont-

real in cars, crossed the river, arrived at St. Albans [Vermont] in the evening, left in morning for Vergennes. Stayed at Vergennes over Sunday.

He was very pleased with this return to his Vermont beginnings, declaring himself to be "quite interested in the staid old city."

"I left there seventy years ago," he wrote, "when I was eleven years old, and could tell the people more of the old city of 70 years past than any person I saw there. The city seems healthy and prosperous, but not one whit larger than when I left in 1814."

On October 20, he and his son boarded a small steamer for the trip down Otter Creek to Lake Champlain, which they then crossed to Westport, New York, from there taking the train to Schenectady via Ticonderoga and Saratoga, and finally home.

Throughout the trip Judson had been uneasy, since, while they were away, his son Fred—in whom neither father nor grandfather had total confidence—was taking the bar exam. As it turned out, Fred passed with honors, but this did not assuage his grandfather's fears. "I trust all will be well with him," said Bennett. "Don't know as he has all the alledged [sic] qualifications."

In November 1884 Jane left for a two-month stay in Chicago ("round trip on Erie R.R. $11.00," noted Joseph), and 26-year-old Belle took over management of the household for her grandfather.[68] Two months later, amid several appreciative comments regarding the quality of the winter's sleighing, which lasted into late March, he noted with pleasure a visit from his congregation. "A large number of members of the Church and Sabbath school came here this evening," he commented on January 29, "an entire surprise. A very good visit. I was presented with a Christmas present, *The Travels and Explorations in Bible Lands*. A memento of their kind regards for their old Sabbath superintendant [sic] and teacher."

---

[68] The journal says that Jane's trip occurred in October. Internal evidence suggests November.

# Joseph Bennett

On April 16, 1885, normally a dangerous time of the year to venture onto Lake Erie ice, the octogenarian reported that he and his hired man had walked more than two miles out onto the lake and found the ice "two feet thick and *solid.*"

In the spring of 1885, following the previous year's construction of a pagoda on his property, he reported that he was building on to the north end of the house, a move that would give him much more room for the business. "Can now accommodate one hundred people," he declared.

He went on, "When I stop to think, I am almost ashamed of myself, that, I should *at my age* think of increasing our boarding business. But as we are in, hardly know how to get out."

Ever the realist, he concluded, "There is a way, however, that will relieve me pretty soon, I hope honorably."

Independence Day 1885 kindled memories. "Another anniversary of our National Independance [*sic*] has arrived," he commented.

> I attend the celebration at Angola, and well remember attending 4th of July war meeting in the town of Jay, Essex County, in the year 1814. Most wonderfully exciting day. We were near the seat of war on the frontier about 15 miles from Plattsburg. I was at that time a little drummer boy—drummed at a recruiting station, my recollection is *clear* and *vivid.*

During this summer he and Jane saw at least 90 boarders. "Jane, my daughter, manages bravely," he wrote, "and getting on very finely. Some excitement, *much work*, a little money and some fun."

As 1885 drew to a close, he took stock. "Another year has gone," he noted.

> Just over the threshold into 1886 and what will be to me and my family at my time of life, must look for the end of my life history at any time. I have lived beyond

the age allotted to man already. I am waiting the roll call. Will it be this year? And am I ready. If so, what matters. I have outlived my usefulness pretty much and want to have my lamp trimmed and burning.

He notes here in passing that son Judson had just been elected town supervisor.

As spring turned into summer the boarders appeared and the cycle began anew. Noting that it was the first of June, he complained that he had not attended church since the previous December "in consequence of the trouble in [his] head and ears."

On July 26, 1886, he received news of the death of his sister, 76-year-old Sarah Price, in Michigan. "We had not heard of her sickness," he confided to his journal. "She was the devoted wife of the late Eld. Price, a fond mother, and affectionate sister, a true and consistant [sic] Christian."

As 1887 opened before him, he again commented on being "one year nearer the end." He had had the comfort over the past few months of his grandson Bertie's presence, but he fretted about the 11-year-old's continuing "nervousness." He began complaining of a "lame back." He became more and more sentimental about his family, which he loved dearly. "I think," he said at Christmas, "I have a right to be proud of my family and their families individually. Not a spot or stain upon any of them."

In March 1888, 84-year-old Joseph produced his usual winter weather observation: "Am having a very nice winter here," he commented. "In the middle of March the most severe snow storm ever known in the middle and eastern part of the state. All kinds of locomotion at a stand still, no eastern train for four days, and very nice weather here."

In June he tried to work in his garden but found himself too weak to continue, and was required to take to his bed. He was diagnosed with pneumonia. Immediately a telegram was sent to Thad Seeley, who left Chicago at once and moved in with his father-in-law for a week. The old man must have been feverish: he was later told that he had received his son-in-law "very indifferently."

"In fact," he commented later, "was very stupid and weak."

Due no doubt to the round-the-clock nursing organized by Jane, as well as to the attendance of sons Seymour and Judson and other family members as frequently as possible, and to the love with which he was surrounded, the old man bounced back. "I was one month in bed," he declared, "with two weeks a blank."

Later that year he commented on the healthy and prosperous condition of his far-flung family, and the passing of another year. "Time with me is passing very monotonous," he declared, "and rapidly passing, but little to mark the time."

In the midst of the gradual failure of his senses, he remained the businessman and observer of everyday life. "I have the charge of Mrs. Salisbury's farm," he recorded in January 1889, "and have rented it to Mr. Michael for another year." Then: "Jane bot [sic] a washing machine. Paid $30.00."

People dropped in to visit this optimistic and happy town scion. "Have had the pleasure of Mrs. Bourns society part of the winter," he reported in early 1889, "a very excellent lady, and with society and Church privileges have enjoyed the winter season very much."

He reported that on May 7, his granddaughter Belle, now 31, married Henry O'Hara of Toronto—"a prominent and influential citizen and very much respected." Belle was married at her father Seymour's house, on Abbott Road in Buffalo. "All our family and many friends present," said Joseph, "fine collection of bridal presents and a very enjoyable wedding."

On May 31 the great flood struck Johnstown, Pennsylvania—"the greatest destruction of life that has ever been known 'by the elements' in America," commented Joseph, "also a vast amount of property destroyed."

# Miles to Go

The homestead saw up to 120 boarders that summer, but Joseph had less and less to do with the operation. In July he reported that he was sitting at General Graves's cottage for Mrs. Graves to make his likeness in clay. That same month, his longtime friend Col. Ira Ayer passed away. He was 86, only slightly older than Joseph. "His family were among the first settlers of the Town of Evans," noted Joseph. "In the winter of 1822 . . . I taught a school at Evans Center, and Col. Ayer was one of my scholars. I know of but three of my pupils that are living, of the sixty that attended my school. Such is life."

On his 86th birthday he was invited to General Graves's cottage. "In entering the lawn," he recalled, "I found a select company of ladies and gentlemen awaiting my arrival. Soon a formal address was read in commemoration of the day of my birth and age." The guests signed a copy of the address, presented the birthday celebrant with a silver spoon as a memento, and then unveiled one of the two busts made by Mrs. Graves. The other, he said, had been donated to the Buffalo Historical Society.

Joseph had become somewhat of a legend to his friends and neighbors. "I feel honored above men," he declared.

Ever the observer of his beloved Lake Erie, he noted the absence of ice in the lake in January 1890—"nothing to obstruct navigation." The winter continued warm and mild, with no sleighing all winter, and no ice on the lake.

On April 1, he reported the departure of Mr. Ahlers, his most recent farm manager, with the surprising announcement that he would henceforth manage the farm himself. The spring, however, proved uncooperative for a farmer of any age. "Spring weather much like the winter," he complained, "too wet and cold for farming, terribly backward." The spring weather also made preparations for the coming camping season quite unpleasant.

His only notation during the summer was that it was going "as usual."

# Joseph Bennett

"The usual casulties [*sic*]," he continued, "have come and gone with the year, births, prosperity, sickness, pleasure, death, gone, gone, all gone."

Fred Bennett, who had married a woman named Emma Jones three years previous, lived in Buffalo. "We all attended a New Years at Fred Bennett's," he reported, ". . . a very nice entertainment. Fred and Emma are finely situated."

Bennett's earlier premonition of Fred's personal implosion would prove valid, but not for another few years.

In February 1891 Bennett was taken ill and confined to his room for 13 days. Again, he recovered. He in fact recovered well enough to find a new family (the Gages) to take over the farm and to help Jane manage the camping and boarding operation. The arrangement worked out well, Bennett reporting in the fall that the summer had been "quite prosperous, and everything pleasant and harmonious."

Not one to be kept at home if he could move about, the 88-year-old Joseph left for Chicago in October, finding the Seeleys in good health except for his beloved Bertie, who seemed "in a decline from heart disease." He reported with a touch of disapproval that he had found Josephine involved in land speculation. He toured the grounds of the coming World's Columbian Exposition, built to mark the 400th anniversary of Columbus's arrival in the new world. "We were in Chicago over three weeks," he wrote, "and came home from a very nice and good visit."

Thanksgiving of 1891 was spent at Seymour's, with even the Toronto O'Haras—Belle and Henry—assisting at the celebration.

Despite his years, Joseph did not neglect to make his usual observation on the quality of the winter. As 1892 opened, he reported "fine sleighing during January and most of February."

# Miles to Go

♣

Although Joseph Bennett had seven years left to live, he now entered upon what would be the final leaf of his journal. He noted the passing of his 89th birthday on August 8. "Our boarders and Judson's boarders," he said, "united in presenting me with a very fine chair in the evening of my birth day. A large collection of people in the Pagoda."

He reported up to 100 boarders that summer.

On October 24, 1892, Joseph Bennett made his final journal entries. It is likely that the two items he recorded that day made further recording of his own life appear insignificant. On that date he wrote of the death of 17-year-old Bertie Seeley, noting that Judson and Jane had left immediately for Chicago. Joseph himself was no longer able to travel. "A terribly sad bereavement," he wrote, "to father and mother, brother, and all of us. He was a bright promising young man."

Then, "I am just informed by letter from Jane in Chicago that my brother Alonzo died last week in Michigan, aged 85 years. I am the oldest of ten children, all lived to manhood, some to old age. Three still living, but only for a short time. Life is short, death inevitable."[69]

♣

August 1896 must have been one of those blistering months of which western New Yorkers think wistfully in February, but of which they complain mightily at the time. During that month, on or about his 93rd birthday, when, according to the editor of the *Angola Record*, "everyone was complaining of the heat, and avoiding all

---

[69] Joseph referred to three living children besides himself. The three were Thomas, Valentine, and Caroline, all of whom would live into the first decade of the new century. It appears that Rhoda and Lucina had predeceased Joseph, although his journal does not mention their deaths. Bennett's youngest daughter Josephine and her husband Thaddeus would both predecease Joseph, the former dying in 1896 and the latter in 1898.

physical effort," Bennett was out walking. After "quite a walk," he found the editor seated on his shady verandah and came up to join him. "I wonder what in the world it means," he said as he settled into a chair. "I feel lazy, just like an old man. Queer, isn't it? What do you suppose is the matter?"[70]

♧

On October 9, 1899, less than three months shy of the new century's dawning, Joseph Bennett was lying on his bed, a little indisposed, chatting quietly with those around him. At 4 PM he died.

On October 12, following funeral services from the homestead and from the Baptist Church at Evans Center—Bishop A.S. Coates, D.D., of Buffalo, presiding—he was buried alongside his beloved wife Mary and daughter Henrietta in the Forest Avenue cemetery in Angola.

A comforting light had been extinguished.

---

[70] *Angola Record*, August 13, 1896.

# AFTERWORD

Joseph Bennett passed on in 1899, but, in the ensuing years, his family—like water running downhill—found its way into communities throughout North America and perhaps beyond. His beloved land remains, no longer farmland, but not changed overmuch since his death.

As has been mentioned, only three of Bennett's siblings were alive in 1892, the year of his final journal entries. These were Thomas, Valentine, and Caroline. Thomas had moved early in life to Oregon, married, and died there in 1903. Valentine, a physician who resided at various times in California, Michigan, and New Jersey, died in 1905, probably in Michigan.[71]  Caroline, as of 1900, was living with her husband in Kansas. It is not known when she died.

As has also been mentioned, two of Bennett's children, Henrietta and Josephine, predeceased him. His daughter Jane, his faithful helpmate for more than 20 years, died in 1916 without issue. Henrietta had also died without issue. Of his five children, only Seymour, Judson, and Josephine had children.

With his first wife, Susan Barton, Seymour had one child, Susan Isabella, or Belle. He had no children with his second wife, Aurelia Coryell.[72]  Seymour died in 1910.

Seymour's daughter Belle and her husband, Henry O'Hara, of Toronto, had three children: Lilian Bennett,

---

[71] Joseph C. Anderson II, of Dallas—the annotator of Bennett's journal mentioned in the Preface—is Valentine's great-great-grandson, descended through Valentine's only daughter Achsah Adelaide.

[72] Aurelia is referred to as Lillie by Joseph, and, as mentioned earlier, she is called variously Coryell and Curry.

born in 1890; Seymour Bennett, born in 1892; and Marion Isabel, born in 1898, all in Toronto.[73]  Lilian married Robert Wilson Carr in 1916, and with him bore four children, the youngest of whom, David Ritchie, was kind enough to supply family photos for this book. Seymour married Dorothy Warren and then (in 1936) Mina Tweedie. With his first wife he had three children, and with his second wife one. Marion, with her husband John Percival Crysdale, had seven children, the youngest of whom was born in 1946.

Judson Bennett, Joseph and Mary's youngest son, married Nancy Taylor in 1861. The couple had one son, Fred, who in 1887 married Emma Jones. Fred and Emma had one child, Grace Louise, born in 1891 in New York. Shortly after Grace's birth, Fred abandoned his family and never returned. In 1929, Grace, after attending Cornell University, married John Moyer, whom she had met in Montana, taking up ranching with him in western Montana. Following her divorce from Moyer in the late 1930s, Grace married John Barnett. *The History of Glacier County, Montana* contains an article on Grace, along with her picture, attesting to her influence in the region. Grace died in 1984.

Judson passed away prior to his elder brother, in 1906. He had been confined to a wheel chair for several years before.

Josephine was the Bennetts' youngest child. With her husband, Thaddeus Seeley, she bore three children, of whom—as is described in the journal—two (Mamie and Bertie) died young. The eldest of these children, Alfred, or Allie, never married. Following the deaths of his parents in the late 1890s, he lived first with his Uncle Seymour, and, following Seymour's death in 1910, with his Aunt Jane (in Hamburg). He is listed in the 1910 census as a news dealer. In the years following Bennett's death he was responsible for publishing a number of postcards featuring the Bennett homestead. David Carr states that

---

[73] Henry also had three children from a previous marriage.

his elder sister Madeleine remembered Allie as a "keen and decent chap whose life was unfortunately restricted by epilepsy." Allie Seeley died in 1932.

♧

As has been mentioned, sometime before 1880 Joseph transferred 50 acres of his 189-acre farm—just above the mouth of Big Sister Creek—to his son Judson, who first established on this land a home and campground called The Bluffs and later a vacation hotel known as Pine Lodge. Judson, who also served a term as town supervisor and maintained a job as Customs Inspector at the Port of Buffalo, ran this facility until his death in 1906. Others ran it after him, well into the 1920s. At the very mouth of the creek was Stevenson's camp. Each facility was served by a high bridge across the creek, used also by residents of Joseph's property further upstream when floodwaters inundated the upstream bridges.

Also prior to 1880, Joseph sold five lakefront acres at the opposite, i.e., southwestern, end of his property to Hiram Backus, who in turn made available 99-year leases to anyone who wished to construct a vacation home on this land. The area soon became known as The Grove, or, like the water on which it touched, Lake Bay. Backus, a colorful entrepreneur, also owned five acres on the opposite side of the Lake Shore Road, in the direction of present-day Beach Road. In 1906 he turned this into a tourist attraction called Wigwam City, where people paid to live in straw-thatched shelters and watch Hi sit atop a pole communicating with his grandmother on Mars.

At some point, possibly as a result of the settlement of Joseph's estate, Seymour took possession of the 15 hilly and wooded lakefront acres immediately south and west of the homestead property, and began to construct cottages and a three-story hotel there. The property was called Bennett Park, and the hotel Bennett Park Villa. By 1906, on Bennett's former land across the road from Lake Bay, an amusement park, replete with Ferris wheel,

177

carousel, circle swing, penny arcade, scenic trolley railroad, and large dance hall, had been constructed. With the opening of trolley service from Buffalo to Angola in 1908 (a 40-minute trip), this operation likely turned a tidy summertime profit. In my own youth this still-popular entertainment destination was known as Lalle's Park.

The District 12 schoolhouse occupied a parcel across the Lake Shore Road from the entrance to Bennett Park, adjoining the site of today's Erie County District 2 Wastewater Treatment Plant. This one-room schoolhouse, which I attended for three years in the 1940s, and which was used as a family residence for many years thereafter, was razed in the 1990s.

It is unknown what became of the Bennett Park operation following Seymour's death in 1910, but by 1921 the facility was owned by John B. Corcoran, and had been renamed Woodcrest Beach, with 15 cottages, space for 25 tents, and plans (never fulfilled) for a nine-hole golf course. Bennett Park Villa was at this time renamed the Woodcrest Beach Hotel. In the late 1920s the Catholic Diocese of Buffalo purchased the Woodcrest Beach property and converted it into a facility for youth camping called the St. Vincent de Paul Camp. It is in use for this purpose to this day.[74] With my brother, sister, and parents, I lived for nine years on this property, my father serving during that period as camp director and caretaker.

In 1923 the homestead property itself—the center of Bennett's world for seven decades—was purchased by the City of Buffalo for $75,000 for use as a park and bathing beach. Known locally in my youth as Buffalo Beach, the park is today called Bennett Beach, and is operated by Erie County. Bennett's home, occupied for many decades after his death by property caretakers,

---

[74] As of this writing, the former Bennett Park Villa and Woodcrest Beach Hotel is still standing. The St. Vincent de Paul Society has slated the structure for demolition in the near future.

was, in the 1980s, adjudged by the county to be too expensive to maintain or refurbish, and was razed.

♧

One can stand on the well beloved, once bustling, but now empty site of Joseph Bennett's homestead, watching the quiet waters of Big Sister Creek drift lakeward, and try to feel the past.

But it can't be brought back.

Like Joseph Bennett and his days, nearly every vestige has been erased, and we must be satisfied with watching leaves fall upon the silent water.

BENNETT HOMESTEAD, ABOUT 1908 – Joseph's family continued the boarding and camping business after his death in 1899. This photo, the original of which is in color, comes from a series of photos of the Bennett property that were hand-tinted in Germany and published as postcards.

TENTS AT BENNETT HOMESTEAD, ABOUT 1908 – In addition to the enjoyment of one of western New York's most pleasant beaches, all guests—whether in cottages or tents—could avail themselves of sporting activities such as baseball, canoeing, rowing, or fishing, and cultural activities such as concerts. Only persons "properly introduced" were welcome to stay at the homestead.

COTTAGE AT BENNETT HOMESTEAD, EARLY 1900s – Public transportation (by 1908, both trolley and train service between Buffalo and Angola) was good enough that a breadwinner could spend time with his family summering in Evans, and still hold down a job in the city.

*Courtesy Town of Evans Historical Society*

BOATING ON BIG SISTER CREEK, 1908 – The creek, popular with canoeists as well as the pictured rowers, carried considerably more water than it does today, and today's creek runs parallel and much closer to the background fenceline.

*Courtesy Town of Evans Historical Society*

VIEW ALONG THE RIDGE FROM THE DINING ROOM – Photo likely taken in 1908. The Bennett homestead brought vacationers to Evans by train from all over western New York and beyond. Note "street" and street lamp. The area stands empty today.

PINE LODGE, BUILT BY JUDSON BENNETT IN THE EARLY 1880s – Judson's hotel and campground were built on his father's former land. Both Bennett resorts were considered by the rising middle class of Buffalo and beyond as select places to spend a summer vacation.

ENTRANCE TO BENNETT PARK, ABOUT 1908 – Following Joseph Bennett's death, Seymour Bennett converted this land—part of his father's original farm purchase—to a resort. As it was then, the property today is distinguished by sturdy stands of hardwood and hemlock. Bennett Park Villa is seen at the top of the hill, the Lake Shore Road in the foreground. The site has been used as a summer camp for children since the late 1920s.

# ACKNOWLEDGMENTS

I am indebted first of all, and most of all, to Joseph C. Anderson II of Dallas, Texas, a great-great-grandson of Joseph Bennett's brother Valentine, for so kindly making available the fruit of his genealogical and other research on Joseph Bennett and his family, as well as for shipping me a photocopy of Bennett's handwritten journal. My work was made immeasurably easier and the treatment rendered fuller by Mr. Anderson's kindness. Due to the ubiquity in this account of references to dates of birth, death, and marriage of Bennett family members and others, I have not footnoted sources of such information, but I will state here that virtually all such data came from Mr. Anderson's research. I thank him warmly for his assistance and support.

Secondly a word of thanks is due to Joseph Bennett's great-great-grandson, David Ritchie Carr of Toronto, Ontario, and to Mr. Carr's son-in-law Craig Laferrière, of Mississauga, Ontario, for their kindness in making available photos of Bennett and other members of the Bennett family. It was Mr. Carr also who put me in touch with Joseph C. Anderson II. I truly appreciate their help and good wishes for this project.

Locally, I'd like to thank Cheryl Delano, Town of Evans Historian, for making available the resources of the Town of Evans Historical Society, and for her comments on the manuscript. Thanks also to James Swinnerton and Karen Connors Erickson for their reading of the material and enthusiastic endorsement of the project. A special word of thanks is due my brother Tim Siepel, for his in-depth and constructive criticism of the manuscript, and to Civil War scholar Ben Maryniak for his critique of material related to the Civil War. I thank Pat Virgil and her staff at the Buffalo and Erie County Historical Society for their patience in digging out well buried materials.

My gratitude to Col. David Fitz-Enz for use of his material on the Battle of Plattsburgh, to the Battle of Plattsburgh Association for use of the Davidson painting of the battle, and to the Chittenango Landing Canal Boat Museum for permission to use two paintings by Dr. Robert E. Hager. Thanks to Dr. Galen Frysinger for making available high-resolution images of the two Hager paintings, and to Cartography Associates for permission to use two maps from the David Rumsey Map Collection. Thanks also to David Leising, grandson of John B. Corcoran and a current resident of Joseph Bennett's former property, for verifying data on his grandfather's ownership of Woodcrest Beach.

Finally, thanks to my wife, Maria Carmen (a Spanish lady who likes to talk) for letting me spend so many hours communing with just a computer.

# SELECTED SOURCES

The primary source for this book was Joseph Bennett's journal, the original of which is owned by the Buffalo and Erie County Historical Society, and typescripts of which may be consulted through the Town of Evans Historical Society.

Other major sources consulted, and valuable resources for anyone interested in the history of Buffalo or Erie County, are as follows:

Beers, Frederick W. *Illustrated Historical Atlas of Erie County, New York.* New York: F.W. Beers Company, 1880.

Johnson, Crisfield. *Centennial History of Erie County, New York.* Buffalo: Matthews & Warren, 1876.

Severance, Frank H., ed. *The Picture Book of Earlier Buffalo.* Buffalo: Buffalo Historical Society, 1912.

Smith, H. Perry, ed. *History of the City of Buffalo and Erie County.* 2 vols. Syracuse: D. Mason & Co., 1884. (available online at http://www.niagara.edu/library/buffhist/eriehome.html)

Turner, Chipman P. *The Pioneer Period of Western New York.* Buffalo: Bigelow Brothers Press, 1888.

White, Truman C., ed. *Our County and its People: A Descriptive Work on Erie County New York.* 2 vols. Boston: The Boston History Company, 1898.

Numerous websites are available to aid the researcher. These may be easily found by means of search engines. Given the dynamic character of the web and the ephemeral nature of URLs, a list of such websites will not be given here.

# INDEX

Black Rock, Village of, 35, 45, 97, 111
Bock, Emil, 149
Boston, Town of, 55, 56, 105
Brant, Town of, 119
Buffalo and Attica railroad, 97, 115
Buffalo Creek reservation, 34, 84
Buffalo, burning of, 1813, 32
Buffalo, Village or City of, xiv, 17, 26, 27, 28, 29, 30, 32,
    35, 36, 39, 44, 45, 49, 50, 52, 53, 57, 58, 59, 80, 84,
    85, 86, 90, 91, 93, 94, 95, 96, 97, 98, 100, 101, 102,
    103, 104, 105, 106, 107, 108, 111, 113, 114, 115,
    116, 117, 118, 119, 120, 121, 122, 124, 125, 126,
    127, 132, 133, 135, 137, 138, 139, 145, 147, 148,
    150, 152, 153, 155, 156, 158, 160, 162, 170, 171,
    172, 177, 178, 182, 184, 185, 187
Butler, Eliza Dibble, 118, 121
Butler, Lizzie, 121
Buxton, Dr. Luther, 119
Carr, David Ritchie, 1, 144, 176, 185
Carr, Robert Wilson, 176
Carrier, Willis, xiii, 80
Cash, Whiting, 48, 150
Cayuga Lake, 23, 24, 25, 49, 95
Chapin, Col. Edward P., 133, 134
Chestnut Ridge, 55, 56
Chicago fire, 156
Cholera epidemics, 93, 102, 128
Clarence Hollow, 34, 35, 37
Clark, John, 161, 164
Cleveland, Pres. Grover, 127
Clinton, De Witt, 44, 59
Coates, Bishop A.S., 174
Collins, Town of, 105, 106
Concord, Town of, 106
Corcoran, John B., 178
Crysdale, John Percival, 176
Curry (Coryell), Aurelia, 147, 148, 175
*Dacotah*, wreck of, 124–25
Dauphin County, Pennsylvania, 65, 87

Senecas, 32, 35
Severance, Charles C., 105, 106, 187
Springville, Village of, 105, 106
St. Vincent de Paul Camp, 178
State Normal School, 109
Sturgeon Point, 38, 113, 116
Superintendents of the Poor, 122, 123, 127, 130, 131, 135
Sweetland, Dr. George, 39, 60, 146, 157, 164
Sweetland, Emma Salisbury, 119
Sweetland, George, Jr., 119, 157
Thayers, 51, 52, 54, 55, 56, 57, 58
   hanging of, 58
Thompson, James, 119
Tonawanda, Town of, 34, 57, 97, 123
Tracy, Albert H., 26, 104, 105
Tweedie, Mina, 176
Union Springs, Village of, 23, 24, 25, 40, 67, 105
University of Buffalo medical school, 95
van Duzer, William, 60
Wallace, William, 115, 116
Warren, Dorothy, 176
Washington Street Baptist Church, 94, 95, 141
Wendt Beach, 30
Weston, Edward Payson, 149, 150
Wilkeson, Judge Samuel, 45
Williams brothers, 24, 26, 28
Williamsville, Village of, 27, 28, 34, 35, 40, 105, 128
Woodcrest Beach, 178
Woodcrest Beach Hotel, 178
Youngs, Jasper B., 108

*Our days are precious but we gladly see them going*
*If in their place we find a thing more precious growing:*
*A rare, exotic plant, our gardener's heart delighting;*
*A child whom we are teaching, a booklet we are writing.*

Hermann Hesse, *Magister Ludi*